200 TIPS
for Growing
Beautiful
Roses

Barbara Blossom Ashmun

CHICAGO
REVIEW
PRESS

Library of Congress
Cataloging-in-Publication Data

Ashmun, Barbara Blossom.
  200 tips for growing beautiful roses / by
Barbara Blossom Ashmun.
     p.   c.
Includes bibliographical references and index.
ISBN 1-55652-277-0 (alk. paper)
  1. Roses.   2. Rose culture.   I. Title.
SB411.A85   1998
635.9'33734–dc21   97-15721
                                                    CIP

©1998 by Barbara Blossom Ashmun
All rights reserved
Published by Chicago Review Press,
Incorporated
814 North Franklin Street
Chicago, Illinois 60610
ISBN 1-55652-277-0
Printed in the United States of America
5 4 3 2 1

In loving memory of my mother,
Anne Nemerow

Contents

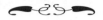

Introduction

My love affair with roses goes back to childhood. At four I was a flower girl at my Aunt Rose's and Uncle Jack's wedding, and that was the first time I touched silky pink rose petals. I reached into the small wicker basket they were nestled in and sprinkled them on the dark red carpet ahead of the bride in her satin gown. It was my first whiff of rose perfume, and I think it bewitched me—when I reached the chuppah the basket was still nearly full and I realized I had fallen down on the job.

In New York City, where I grew up, roses came from florists, cost the earth, and signified a special occasion. It wasn't until I moved to Portland, OR, in 1972 that I had a chance to grow my own roses, and actually one of Portland's many attractions was that I'd heard it was called the City of Roses. The first house I lived in had a bed of overgrown hybrid teas along the front path that were a perpetual thorn in the mailman's side. But to me, they were magic—how else could a bundle of prickly sticks explode into fragrant roses?

Like most novice gardeners, I began with hybrid tea roses. I nearly fainted when my neighbor pruned them for me. She whacked the canes off two feet from the ground, and I was sure they were demolished forever. But no, they grew like crazy, and the mailman was grateful—now they stayed under five feet and he could get by without being snagged.

I saw my first old roses on a visit to Victoria, B.C. I still remember the sumptuous pink, cup-shaped flowers of 'Reine Victoria', a Bourbon rose, in Brent Webber's garden. At Shirley Beach's garden next door, climbing roses covered wide arches just like at Monet's Giverny. On a trip to Seattle I visited Voni Artiano's garden in Mukilteo, where an arbor was smothered with fragrant pink roses—that was my introduction to 'Belle Amour', a vigorous alba rose. I had to have it—now it climbs an old pear tree in my own garden. Voni invited me to sniff 'Agnes', an unusual yellow rugosa rose, and its scent lured me to grow rugosas. The door had opened to a whole new world of heritage roses, and I soon began ordering them sight unseen from Canadian catalogs.

In the seventies and eighties, old roses were scarce in Portland's nurseries, and mail order was the only way to acquire them. But in 1986 Heirloom Old Garden Roses opened in St. Paul, Oregon, and gardeners began a round of steady pilgrimages to study and buy roses on their own roots. Over the years John and Louise Clements have developed a never-ending series of demonstration gardens that show how to grow roses of every kind over arbors, up trellises, onto fences, and in beds and borders.

In the summer of 1986 I toured English gardens and marveled at the vast array of roses that were common there but new and exotic to me. Soon afterward I moved from a city garden to two-thirds of an acre, where I could experiment with roses and perennials to my heart's content. As a garden designer I felt it was my responsibility to know their growth habits and become well acquainted with their exact colors and scents—what better excuse to indulge in rose-buying sprees without guilt? Education has always been a priority in my family, and how better to know roses than to grow them?

Wherever rose workshops or conferences were offered, I went—to California, to Washington, to Canada, and even to New Zealand. When I heard of a rose society that could teach me about roses,

I joined. With so many roses to learn about, I figured I could use all the help I could get. Now, when I come across my old notes from lectures, I realize I could have benefited from a crash course in German and French too, to properly spell those rose names, but phonetic spelling was a good start.

Fortunately, the study of roses never ends—every year, catalogs explode with new introductions. Designing with roses is an ongoing education too—our infinite imaginations are always ready to dream up new and unexpected compositions with roses and companion plants. Each season we get out our spades and improve the garden just a little more. The process is so much fun we'd hate to reach perfection.

This small book is a collection of tips to accompany you on your adventure with roses, and to encourage you to sample widely from the rich selections. Roses give you color longer than any other genus and offer you flowers in such a variety of shapes, colors, and scents that it's almost hard to believe that they're all related. I invite you to try as many as you have room for and wish for you the great pleasure that they've brought to me.

Acknowledgments

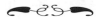

Without the growers, where would we be? Deprived, covetous, and wanting. My deepest appreciation goes to all the nurseries that supply us with our beauties, especially Heirloom Old Garden Roses in St. Paul, Oregon, a combination rose university and rose candy store. John and Louise Clements and their family and staff have been very generous in sharing their knowledge of roses–their enthusiasm is contagious.

Many friends have taught me and shared tips, slips, and trips. I thank Sandy Childress for sharing our many rose-hunting expeditions and appreciate her willingness to make room in The Green Moose for all those plants, even when most of them were mine. Loie Benedict gave me my first rugosa rose slip–it was 'Blanc Double de Couvert', which grew into a fragrant colony. Alice Frazer bestowed a vanload of old roses on me, which Mary Eggebraatten dug and delivered one miserably rainy February day. Those bundles of sticks turned out to be the glorious 'Madame Hardy', 'Celestial', and 'Alain Blanchard'.

My thanks to the following rose experts, who've advised me about favorite roses for their part of the country, how best to grow them, and solutions to problems they've faced with pests, diseases, and weather: Claire Argast, Portland Nursery, Portland, OR; Dennis Konsmo, Federal Way, WA; Henry Najat, M.D., Monroe, WI; Bob Osborne, Corn Hill Nursery Ltd., Petitcodiac, NB.; Bill Patterson, Roses Unlimited, Laurens, SC; Helen Pressley, Olympia, WA; David Phipps, horticulturist, West Linn, OR; Conrad Tips, Houston, TX; Lily-Shohan, Clinton Corners, NY; Randy Watson, M.D., Portland, OR; Miriam Wilkins, San Francisco, CA; John Wohler, United Horticultural Supply, Portland, OR.

I also appreciate the valuable information culled over the years from membership in the Portland Rose Society, the Heritage Rose Group, and the Hardy Plant Society of Oregon–all the lectures and open gardens were better than going to horticultural graduate school. I salute the many writers and photographers who brought roses of all kinds to my doorstep long before I put a spade in the soil; for my favorite books on roses, please see "Suggested Reading" on page 126.

What Roses Need to Thrive

(1) **When it comes to planting roses, nothing is more important than starting out right with a big planting hole and good soil.** I was shocked at the huge planting holes at a favorite rose nursery, Heirloom Old Garden Roses. My friend Ruth Mackey stepped down into one, and the hole was up to her knees! But when I saw how vigorously their roses grew, I started digging craters too. I dig a hole at least two feet wide by two feet deep. Then I add about six inches of well-rotted compost or aged manure at the bottom of the hole, and a handful of bonemeal. If your soil is clay-based, amend the remainder of the soil with peat moss, more compost, or even recycled potting soil (from old contain-

ers) to improve the texture for better drainage.

2 **To check the drainage of your soil, dig a two-foot hole and fill it with water.** If the water hasn't drained out completely in 24 hours, it's important to improve the drainage before planting. Add at least six inches of gravel, grit, or pumice at the bottom of the hole. Or raise the entire bed 12 inches or more above ground level.

3 **The best fertilizer for the planting hole is well-rotted cow manure or manure from horses fed with alfalfa hay and bedded down on wood shavings.** Cow manure and horse manure are not likely to burn the feeder roots of roses, but rabbit and chicken manure have been known to be too hot for the root zone. However, rabbit and chicken manure work well as a topdressing, spread out in a circle around the trunk of the rose.

Stay away from manure from horses fed with oat hay or straw hay, and avoid manure of horses bedded on oat hay or straw—all of these materials contain seeds that will germinate in your rose borders.

4 **Fertilizer formulas tell you the percentage of nitrogen, phos-**

phorus, and potassium, in that order.
There are so many rose fertilizers on the market, organic and chemical, that choosing one can be very confusing. But whether it's a box of commercial rose food on the supermarket shelf or a sack of bonemeal at the feed store, three numbers tell you what's inside. For example, 15-10-5 means that the material is 15 percent nitrogen, 10 percent phosphorus, and 5 percent potassium. The other 70 percent is filler, so the higher the numbers, the more actual food for the roses.

⑤ Chemical fertilizers release quickly, while organic fertilizers are slower to break down. Chemical fertilizers are manufactured synthetically and break down faster than organic fertilizers, giving plants a quick boost. They are especially beneficial in cool weather when the soil temperature is below 50 degrees. However, because they release quickly, what the plant can't digest leaches back into the water table if you use too much. Follow directions on the box for correct amounts.

Organic fertilizers release nutrients more slowly, allowing the plants to take what they need over time. They're harmless to animals, people, and the environment. However, they're most effective at soil temperatures above 50 degrees, when microbes can convert them into forms available to the plant roots. Also, organic fertilizers usually have smaller amounts of active fertilizer than chemical fertilizer. For example, cottonseed meal has only 7 percent nitrogen, compared to many chemical rose foods that have 15 percent.

Some fertilizer companies are now producing a blend of chemical and organic rose food that covers all the bases—a quick shot of chemical food to start the season off and a slow-release organic to keep the roses well nourished. You could do the same by applying both types of fertilizer at appropriate times.

6 **To promote healthy green leaves and canes, add nitrogen to the soil.** Blood meal, recycled sewage sludge, cottonseed meal, alfalfa, fish emulsion, fish meal, bat guano, poultry manure, and rabbit manure are rich in nitrogen. It's especially important to add nitrogen to the soil if you've mulched the ground with wood products (bark dust, sawdust) that consume nitrogen as they break down. Too much nitrogen may cause your plants to be bigger than is beneficial (plants that get huge are also likely to topple over in rain and wind).

7 **Add phosphorus to the soil to increase flower and hip produc-**

tion and develop strong roots. Bonemeal and phosphate rock are the two highest sources of phosphorus for your garden. I routinely sprinkle bonemeal in the planting hole whenever I plant new roses.

8 **Add potassium for early growth, stem and cane strength, and plant vigor.** Wood ashes, seaweed, hay, guano, granite dust, kelp, alfalfa, and greensand are good sources of potassium. Granite dust and greensand, being mineral, are slower to break down than ashes, seaweed, hay, and guano, their plant and animal counterparts.

9 **To encourage strong growth, feed your roses generously with an organic formula that works wonders.** A friend tried this feeding schedule recommended by a local rose maven, and she enjoyed exceptionally vigorous rosebushes. At the beginning of the season, mix one-half cup blood meal (15-1-1) and one-half cup cottonseed meal (7-2-1) and work into the soil at the base of each rose.

Every three weeks, water your roses with a diluted solution of fish emulsion at the rate of one tablespoon for each gallon. Three times during the growing season, fortify your roses with alfalfa tea. Throw three handfuls of 5-1-2 alfalfa meal or pellets in a garbage can filled with water and let the mixture steep overnight. Water each rose with a gallon or two of this nutritious brew.

10 **Here are two more organic formulas that produce great results:** Mix three parts fish meal, six parts rock phosphate, and six parts greensand in a wheelbarrow, and spread one to two cups around each rosebush. Or mix one cup each of alfalfa meal, bonemeal, fish meal, and gypsum and spread around each rosebush each spring.

11 **Our local rose society sells a chemical fertilizer that's made my roses very happy. Feed established bushes about a cup of a similar mixture in April for terrific bloom.** Here's the formula: 15-10-10 (15 percent nitrogen, 10 percent phosphorus, 10 percent soluble potash), with trace elements added–2 percent magnesium, .1 percent copper, .5 percent iron, .2 percent manganese, and .2 percent zinc.

Roses are heavy feeders, which shouldn't come as a big surprise if you consider how many flowers they produce. In my garden, they have to compete with nearby perennials, annuals, and bulbs for water and fertilizer–in some places I thread clematis through the bushes, adding to the company they keep. To insure a good supply of food I use chemical as well as organic fertilizers, and a topdressing of compost or aged manure.

12 **Give your roses plenty of water for health and good flowering.** Roses need at least one to two inches of water weekly to be content. If you're not sure how much water your sprinklers are delivering, set a shallow empty can in the bed and measure the amount.

Ideally, roses benefit from watering in the morning, and from below (soakers or drip irrigation) to lessen the possibility of fungal disease. Watering late in the day leaves the roses damp overnight, making them more vulnerable to powdery mildew and black spot. However, I learned from a rose grower, much to my surprise, that if you water overhead continuously *all* night, you wash away fungal disease.

13 **Plant roses in spring for more successful results.** Even though the "fall is for planting" motto is used to encourage gardeners to take advantage of autumn's pleasant weather and end-of-season plant sales, if your winters are cold, fall is actually a riskier season for planting roses. I've lost more fall-planted roses than I like to admit—too often inclement weather hits before the new roses have established strong enough root systems to sustain them through the cold and wind. Planting in spring gives the young plants three seasons to develop substantial roots and canes before facing the challenge of a harsh winter.

14 **If you're not sure where to place a new rose, pot it up into an ample container while you're thinking things over.** It's easy to get carried away at the nursery and buy plants before the soil is prepared. You're not alone–most of us have a stash of plants that resembles a mini-nursery sitting on the patio, waiting for a home. Get the roses growing right away by potting them up into generous containers filled with rich potting soil. This is especially important if you've bought bare-root roses, or if your roses are on their own roots in narrow rose pots. Feed these shrubs liquid fish fertilizer or a liquid dilution of a complete fertilizer (always following the directions on the label) every few weeks.

Two- or five-gallon fiber pots are ideal for growing roses this way. When you're ready to plant the roses, cut away the sides and bottom of the pot instead of knocking the rose out of the pot and risking damage to the canes. Even if you've grown your new rose in a large plastic pot, go easy on the plant by cutting the pot apart.

15 **Even though the label may tell you it's OK to plant a rose in its fiber pot, don't.** Pulp pots don't disintegrate quickly enough for the rose roots to push through the bottom—instead they mat at the base of the pot and start circling around, looking for a way out. Cut the pot apart and plant the rose directly in the ground to avoid wasting the rose's energy. Loosen the roots a little by pulling them apart gently before planting.

16 **Most roses flower best with at least six hours of sun daily.** Although some roses bloom well enough in shade (see the chapter headed "Roses for Particular Places"), the majority of roses are sun-lovers. Half a day of sun will suffice, although the same plant in full sun will grow bigger and bloom more.

Shade at the base of trees presents roses with more problems than shade at the base of a wall—tree roots deplete the soil of moisture and fertilizer, so that the ground around their trunks is dry and compacted. It's possible to grow roses in the dappled shade of deciduous trees if you prepare the soil well, water regularly, and mulch.

17 **Mulch roses with compost or well-rotted manure to conserve**

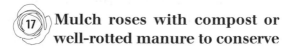

moisture, boost nutrition, and improve the overall texture of the soil. When my garden was new I was thrilled to see the roses survive, but once they established themselves I began mulching them with chicken manure and watched them explode into vigorous growth and bloom. Mushroom compost or homemade compost are also good sources of nutrition for roses.

Perennials have a habit of creeping right up to the rose's trunk, so first clear away those that are smothering the base of the rose, and save them to transplant into other beds. Then pour a generous few inches of chicken manure around the trunk, spreading it evenly at the rose's base. Water thoroughly, letting the sprinklers or soakers run for at least half an hour.

In very warm weather, chicken manure may dry out quickly and form a crust at the top, making it difficult for water to penetrate. If this happens, scratch the manure into the soil gently with a cultivating fork or a hand fork.

18 **To keep weeds away from newly planted roses and to conserve moisture, even a mulch of grass clippings, bark dust, sawdust, or shredded newspaper will help.** Admittedly this is less attractive than nutritious compost or manure, but sometimes we're in a hurry and don't have time to shop for supplies. Any material that will let water through and cover the ground helps to discourage weeds and keep the roots cool and damp. Grass clippings are easily available–your own or your neighbors'–just be sure they haven't been sprayed with herbicide. Studies have shown that residual herbicide from lawn clippings harms perennials and annuals.

Be aware that as wood-based mulches break down they use up nitrogen, so compensate for this by added some fertilizer high in nitrogen underneath the mulch.

(19) Thorough cleanup and a dormant spray applied early in the season (before the roses leaf out) will cut your disease problems in half. First be sure to clean up any of last year's leaves that might be sitting on the ground–they can be infected with powdery mildew, rust, or black spot spores. Then thoroughly spray your rose canes with a dormant spray that combines horticultural oil and lime sulfur to smother insect eggs and fungicidal spores. Spray the ground underneath the roses as well, just in case any stray infected leaves are lingering there.

Some growers also recommend a dormant spray in late fall after you strip the old leaves off the rosebushes.

20 **Encourage good air circulation to prevent fungal diseases.** Mildew, black spot, and rust are more likely to flourish where the leaves stay damp for long periods of time–in the shade, where it's cooler, and of course in very rainy climates. Densely growing rose shrubs with congested canes and foliage that's jammed together are more prone to fungal diseases–the leaves tend to stay damp longer.

Freely circulating air dries leaves quickly, promoting a healthy plant. In the spring before the roses leaf out, open rosebushes to allow breezes through by pruning out the small twiggy branches that point toward the center of the bush and by reducing the number of canes.

21 **To combat black spot, rust, and powdery mildew, spray with a baking soda solution for the fewest toxic side effects.** Combine a tablespoon of baking soda and a few drops of soap or mineral oil (to help the solution stick to the leaves) in a gallon of water, and spray weekly with this solution to fight fungal diseases. Be sure to cover the undersides as well as the top surfaces of the leaves when you spray. Regular treatment–every week or so–will make your efforts more effective.

22 **Always read the labels before using fungicides, pesticides, and**

herbicides, and take proper precautions. I usually shy away from sprays that might do as much damage to me as to fungi, insects, and weeds, but once in a long while we all get desperate when there's a serious infestation on a favorite plant. That's when it's important to read the instructions very carefully and follow all precautions, even if you might look silly. Wear waterproof gloves, long sleeves, and a mask to protect yourself. Put your pets in the house—they can easily track through the sprayed area and lick their paws. Spray on a still day so that the wind doesn't shower the wrong plants or send the mist back in your face.

(23) **Test-spray a small area of your rosebush for starters.** Before you get carried away, try out a small amount of spray on the back of the plant just to be sure it's not averse to the solution. Also, be aware that some plants that might be near your roses are sensitive even to soapy solutions. Sweet peas, begonias, bleeding hearts, fuchsias, gardenias, some ferns, lantanas, and Japanese maples have been reported to react adversely to liquid soap.

(24) **Early prevention is the best cure for fungal diseases.** As soon as you see signs of disease, pick off the affected leaves and discard them in the

garbage. Do the same in the fall, cleaning up diseased leaves so that the spores don't winter over and spread. In the spring, spray roses likely to be susceptible with a dormant oil spray.

Some roses are more susceptible to diseases than others. Your particular climate and soil as well as the nature of the rose play a part in plant health. In my rainy Pacific Northwest garden, I can count on many Bourbon and hybrid perpetual roses to have black spot every spring. Steady rain in March, April, and May makes it nearly impossible to find an opportunity to spray, complicating the problem. My solution is to grow fewer Bourbons and more disease-resistant hybrid musk and shrub roses.

(25) Whatever you spray, do it when the temperature is cool, early in the morning or late in the evening. Whether you're spraying liquid fertilizer, fungicide, or pesticide, avoid spraying in the heat of the day. Direct sun on freshly sprayed leaves can burn the foliage. It's also a good idea to water your plants well the day before spraying so that they're not stressed. Avoid spraying on windy days when you will have little control over your target.

(26) Before reaching for toxic pesticides, look for a safer solution.

Most pesticides don't discriminate between bad bugs and good bugs, and
some can harm people and animals too.
Not only that, but many "problem" bugs
such as aphids are also a food source
for birds and beneficial insects such as
ladybugs and lacewings. Often if you let
nature take its course, the good guys will
eat the bad guys for dinner.

Before you spray, ask yourself–Is this
insect really a threat to my roses? Spit
bugs might be unattractive but they do
no damage. Although aphids are more
destructive, I know from experience that
shortly after they appear, the ladybugs
arrive to feast. Try knocking aphids off
the roses with a stream of water strong
enough to wash them away but not so
forceful that the new buds get decapi-
tated. If this mild step isn't effective
enough, spray with an insecticidal soap,
following directions on the label.

27 **For your own health, the health
of your family, friends, pets,
and the environment, control insects
mechanically instead of chemically.**
Hand picking the larger insects is both
satisfying and safe. If you're squeamish,
slip on a pair of surgical gloves before
you go hunting. Early in the morning
and late in the evening are the best
times. Fill an old milk jug with water
mixed with a little Clorox or ammo-
nia, gather up slugs and snails, and

plunk them in. Shake beetles and ear-wigs out of the roses and into your container. This is a very relaxing activity that will give a strong feeling of accomplishment without any worry about breathing in poisonous fumes.

28 **Discourage deer with fencing, human urine, or surprising showers.** In New Zealand, where the deer problem is intense, many of the rose gardens I visited were guarded by 10-to-12-foot post and wire fences, which were used very effectively to train rambling roses.

Liz Druitt, in her book *The Organic Rose Garden*, recommends applying human urine full strength around the boundaries of your garden and diluted around the roses—organic, economical, and earthy.

An innovative gardener I know hooked her irrigation system up to a light sensor. When the deer came visiting they triggered the sprinklers and were startled enough to depart.

29 **If your winter temperatures are below 20 degrees for long periods without the benefit of snow cover, protect your roses from the cold.** Many methods are used by avid rose growers protect roses from freezing. After the first frost a foot or two of mulch can be piled up at the base of the plant, to be removed in the spring. For harsh climates, ready-made Styrofoam cones can be purchased and slipped over the whole bush.

Some folks construct a four-foot-tall circular frame of chicken wire or hardware cloth or use a square tomato cage (the kind that folds away for easy storage), then fill these structures with leaves, shredded bark, dirt, or straw for insulation. Several thicknesses of newspaper can be stapled together to make the frame–ditto with bubble-wrap, old carpet pads, or old carpets. Boxes with lids can be constructed from exterior plywood, then disassembled and stored for reuse.

Lop canes back to fit them into these enclosures, and tie them together to make the shrub more compact. If the structure has a top, don't close it until the temperature turns very cold, and open it again on warm winter days as needed.

30 **In very cold climates (below 0 degrees for long periods) grow very winter-hardy roses.** Rugosas, hybrid rugosas, albas, damasks, and spinosissima roses adapt well to cold climates. 'Therese Bugnet' is one of the hardiest rugosas (to zone 2), with double lavender-pink flowers on a tall, upright shrub that is tolerant of partial shade. The Canadian Explorer roses are especially tough, with 'William Baffin' at the top of the list. Distinguished by deep pink semidouble flowers brushed with white and showy golden stamens, this vigorous rose may be grown as a shrub or trained as a climber. 'John Cabot', with darker rose-pink blossoms, is another tough Canadian rose that does double duty as a shrub or climber.

(31) Protect your roses from icy winds. Keeping the beds well watered helps to insulate the roots and prevents the canes from dessicating in cold, drying winter winds. Some growers recommend spraying the canes with an antitranspirant.

Where winds are an ongoing problem, plant hedgerows of wind-resistant plants, or build a wall to modify your climate. One of my favorite gardens in the Columbia River Gorge is well protected from wind by a towering hedge of evergreen incense cedar; another windy garden in McMinnville is protected by hedges of *Rosa californica plena*, a beautiful species rose with fragrant pink flowers. Check with your local nursery for the best windbreak plants for your particular area.

(32) To protect roses from winter damage, stop fertilizing by the

end of August. Fertilizing roses too late in summer and fall promotes tender growth that is more vulnerable to cold damage. In some cases it can also make your plants so tall that they blow around in the wind, and then the crown loosens from the soil and the roots get exposed to cold. Cut back any roses that are too tall by about one-third to prevent the wind from whipping them around, and top-dress the crowns with aged compost.

(33) **During the spring and summer, when a rose gets too heavy suddenly, prop it up with tree prunings.** Sometimes a particularly rainy and warm year will send a rose into unusually vigorous growth. This happened recently in my garden when 'Honorine de Brabant', a Bourbon that for the last six years stood upright on its own with no support, suddenly burgeoned outlandishly. So did *Clematis* 'Etoile Violette' that I had threaded through the rose's canes, adding to the weight. Winter flooding and a record spring rainfall probably caused this unusual growth spurt.

To keep its newly enormous flower-laden branches from breaking, I slid several large branches that had been pruned off an old apple tree under the lower canes. I grabbed the rose canes with the forked parts of the apple branches, snagging the prickly canes and lifting them up off the ground. Then I jammed the lower, straight ends of the apple stakes into the ground at a slight angle, adjusting them so that they held enough tension to prop up and support the rose canes. (This job is best done by lying belly-down on the ground at the base of the rosebush, breathing deeply, and staying alert so as not to get ambushed by thorns.)

34 Remove suckering branches from grafted roses. When you least expect it, a strange cane shoots up from the base of a grafted rose with leaves of a different color green and a different shape than the rest of the plant. This is the understock trying to assert itself and become a rose. Don't let it. Dig down below the ground and find the place where the sucker has sprung from the root. Cut it off flush with the root with sharp pruners or a knife.

Once this suckering begins, it's likely to repeat, so keep an eye out for this different kind of growth, and cut it out as soon as you spot it.

35 To avoid suckering and freezing of the graft union, grow own-root roses. Own-root roses are grown as vegetative cuttings from a mother plant. They won't suffer from the problem many grafted roses experience in very cold winters, when the graft union freezes, the rose itself dies, and the understock is what remains to bloom the following spring. Many of us end up with a lot of dark red 'Dr. Huey' roses after a severe winter, not what we had in mind. Own-root roses, on the other hand, even if frozen back in a hard winter, will most always return from their roots (the exception being roses planted very late in the fall that are not well established before a freeze.)

With no understock, own-root roses aren't marred by understock suckering. However, they may run on their own roots and spread further than you like. That's the time to dig out the runners and pot them up for a friend.

So Many Kinds of Rose Flowers

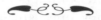

36 **Single roses are especially strik-ing—their display of stamens adds an elegant detail to the flower, and some have an arresting eye of a contrasting color.** Single roses have from five to seven petals arranged in a single row. The simplicity of single flow-ers is refreshing. Most have a central boss of yellow stamens, especially showy when contrasted with red pet-als, as in 'Scharlachglut' ('Scarlet Fire') or 'Dortmund', both shrub roses that may be trained to climb. 'Dortmund' has the added excitement of a white eye at the center of its ruffled red flowers.

Even more unusual are the single flowers with dark burgundy stamens at their centers: 'Dainty Bess', an older pink hybrid tea introduced in 1925, and 'White Wings', bred from 'Dainty Bess'.

Pink-flowering 'Dapple Dawn', creamy white 'Wild Flower', and 'Red Coat' are three of David Austin's lovely English roses with single flowers. 'Complicata', a once-blooming brilliant pink gallica that I can't live without, and 'Nevada', a white shrub rose, are both showstoppers in bloom.

Too many of the species roses to mention are single flowered, so I'll just make special note of three favorite single hybrid rugosas: 'Fru Dagmar Hastrup', with immense single pink fragrant flowers followed by showy hips; 'Robusta', with gorgeous red blooms; and 'Scabrosa', fragrant and pink.

(37) Semidouble flowers have 8 to 20 petals arranged in two or three rows. Like the single roses, semidoubles open wide enough to show their stamens, but they have more petals than the singles. They're right in between simple and sumptuous, with a relaxed informality that allows them to blend very nicely with perennials and annuals in a mixed border.

Pinkish red 'Vanity' and white 'Moonlight' are two terrific hybrid musk roses with semidouble flowers. 'Apothecary's Rose', also known as the red rose of Lancaster (*Rosa gallica officinalis*), is a long-blooming old rose with delicious fragrance. Delicate pink 'Escapade' is a favorite semidouble floribunda rose with a sweet, old-fashioned look.

38 Double roses have 21 or more petals and come in a wide variety of shapes. It amazes me that such huge flowers can emerge from deceptively small buds. Voluptuous big double roses such as David Austin's pink-red 'Wenlock' sometimes get so heavy with petals that they bend their own stems. When 'Empress Josephine', a double pink gallica, blooms, the weight of its flowers pulls the canes into a garland. The same arching effect graces the garden when 'La Ville de Bruxelles', a damask, offers its very double, fragrant pink flowers.

39 Choose at least a few quartered roses to enjoy their unusually alluring design. Double roses that are quartered are among the most beautiful—their inner petals are folded into four symmetrical compartments, making a very pleasing pattern. 'Königin von Dänemark', a fragrant pink alba rose that dates back to 1826; 'Charles de Mills', a purplish pink scented gallica; and 'Duchesse de Montebello', a fragrant, shell pink gallica are good examples of delightfully quartered roses. For the most part, quartered roses have flat faces, the better to show off gorgeous petals and waft their perfume.

40 **A few choice double roses show a green button eye when fully open.** Like an exclamation point, the green button eye at the center of an opulent rose is just a little extra embellishment for us to enjoy. 'Madame Hardy', a choice white damask, enjoys this delightful detail. So does pink 'Fantin-Latour', a robust centifolia, and light pink lightening to white 'Madame Zoetmans', a compact damask.

41 **For a romantic garden, select some cupped roses too.** Gracefully shaped cupped roses look very rounded, like a goblet. Many of the fragrant Bourbon roses have this shape, especially 'La Reine Victoria', a delightful rich pink, and its pastel pink sport, 'Madame Pierre Oger'. There is something irresistibly charming about the way the gracefully recurving outer petals surround and embrace the many inner petals.

42 **Grow some roses with fringed petals, and plant some cottage pinks (*Dianthus plumarius*) nearby**

to mimic the roses. It's fun to grow roses that are a little different, and why not add some cottage pinks nearby to echo the flower shapes? Try 'F. J. Grootendorst', a tall shrubby hybrid rugosa loaded with clusters of small red flowers, or 'Pink Grootendorst'. I take advantage of their height (six to eight feet) to screen my garden from a neighboring motor home.

The only thing they lack is fragrance–planting clove-scented cottage pinks at their feet takes care of that small shortcoming.

(43) For the most intense color display, select roses with clusters of single flowers. Single flowers open wide, and those that bloom in clusters produce large expanses of color. Pink 'Ballerina', 'Red Ballerina', pinkish red 'Mozart', pale pink 'Kathleen', white 'Lyda Rose', and pink 'New Face' are just a few examples of reblooming shrubby roses of this nature. Cream-colored 'Rambling Rector', blue-violet 'Veilchenblau', and many other once-blooming ramblers also fall into this category.

Just for fun I counted over two hundred dainty flowers blooming at the end of a single cane of 'Ballerina'. Imagine how much color you get with such an abundance of flowers.

44 For cut flowers or competing in rose shows, choose the more modern hybrid tea and grandiflora roses. As interest in showing and cutting roses increased, roses were bred for longer petals, producing a larger, more pointed bud and flower. Emphasis was on the beauty of each individual flower–larger flowers with long stems for cutting and more and more brilliant colors appeared on the market. Garden-worthy qualities such as intoxicating scent and graceful form of the entire bush took a backseat.

Consequently the upright, rather stiff form of the hybrid teas and grandifloras makes them difficult to place in the garden–they don't blend well into the flow of beds and borders. Since they also flower best when bedded out on their own without competition from nearby perennials, placing them in a cutting garden of their own or along a sunny driveway with a low edging of annuals is probably the best solution, both horticulturally and aesthetically.

Designing
with Roses

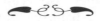

45 The easiest way to create harmony in the garden is to stick with pastel colors. Blending pink, cream, white, and light yellow roses makes for a restful and easygoing color scheme. Adding blue and blue-violet perennials such as speedwell, lavender, or delphinium is sure to please. Pale tones give the garden a feeling of spaciousness, adding light and airiness. Keep in mind that green is always the silent partner, supporting the array of flowers (isn't it lucky that grass and most leaves are green and not red?).

I savored a fine example of a pastel rose border at Heirloom Old Garden Roses nursery in St. Paul, Oregon. A collection of hybrid musk roses were arranged in a semicircle around a fountain. All were in shades of pink, light yellow, and white: 'Ballerina', 'Buff Beauty', 'Thisbe', 'Lavender Lassie', 'Pink Prosperity', 'Prosperity', 'Sally Holmes', 'Felicia', and 'Kathleen'. Bright pink 'Belinda' was the only strong color in the arrangement, and it stood at the midpoint of the semicircle as an exclamation point. Heavenly.

46 To add depth and drama, be sure to include mauve, purple, and dark crimson. Pastels may be safe, but sooner or later we crave the thrill of more intense colors. Fortunately, there are plenty of purple, mauve, and crimson roses to choose from, especially among the gallica, Bourbon, and moss roses. The color of old velvet and water-stained satin, many of these roses bloom reddish purple at first, then evolve into darker purple and eventually grayish lavender in the same way that hydrangea blossoms transform themselves. These changes remind me of the way highly polished copper and brass antiques age, losing their early bright shine to a mellower burnish.

47 If it's at all possible, separate the orange and orange-red roses from the red and purple roses. Bright orange and red-orange both contain yellow, which sets them apart from red and purple roses that contain blue. A clash between the yellow-based reds and blue-based reds is inevitable. Just as you would never invite incompatible friends to the same party, keep warring colors at different ends of the garden, or separate them with a hedge, a fence, or a buffer zone of mediating colors. Blue flowers, gray or blue-green foliage, or even variegated foliage (which translates as cream) will all quiet down the commotion between clashing colors.

(48) Orange and orange-red roses combine well with golden, burgundy, and variegated foliage and yellow, red, orange, and purple flowers. One October evening I came across a glowing garden in the city of Edmonds, Washington. Red roses (possibly 'Scarlet Meidiland') bloomed brilliantly in front of red-stemmed variegated dogwood shrubs (*Cornus alba* 'Elegantissima'). A backdrop of purple-flowering butterfly bushes (*Buddleia davidii*) provided height and fragrance, while orange-red 'Paprika' marigolds and deep yellow coneflowers (*Rudbeckia* 'Goldsturm') added heat at the front of this arrangement. Purple-leaved barberries and New Zealand flax made the picture sizzle.

(49) **Be aware of the ultimate size and shape of a rose to best place it in your garden.** Let the size and shape of a plant serve you rather than create work for you. If you're in love with 'Hansa', a heavily scented rugosa rose blooming brilliant pink-red, keep in mind that it's going to grow at least six feet tall, probably more. Even though you want to enjoy its fragrance, don't place it near an open window because it will probably end up obscuring your light, and keep it away from the path— you will get very cranky when it scratches your arms and snags the mail carrier too. Instead, place it at the back of a flower border where it can stretch to its heart's content and keep out the neighbor's dog.

(50) **Choose roses proportionate to the size of your garden.** As beautiful as the hybrid musk 'Mozart' is—I consider it floral Prozac, with bright red-pink flowers that never fail to cheer me—you must give it eight feet of horizontal space to spread its glorious canes or else you'll be pruning its prickly branches forever. Save yourself this chore if you have a small garden, and choose compact pink 'Felicia' instead. It'll stay nicely contained in a four-foot area, dignified and reserved, with beautiful double pink flowers.

51 Plant draping roses to cascade over the tops of walls and arch gracefully on the banks of a pond. Use the form of naturally weeping roses to advantage: to soften the hard edges and decorate the face of a stone wall or to point to a water feature and add color at the edges. The same shape is useful for containers, raised beds, banks, and rock gardens.

'Raubritter', a once-blooming hybrid macrantha with cupped pink flowers that bloom for months, is perfect for a slope. Mine blooms like a pink petticoat at the base of an enormous white species rose, *Rosa murielae*, and drapes over a carpet of furry gray lamb's ears (*Stachys lanata*). 'The Fairy', a pink reblooming polyantha rose that opens in midsummer and continues, also arches attractively. Shiny leaves and small profuse flowers make it very desirable.

'The Countryman', a double pink English shrub rose with large, recurrent flowers, also leans gracefully. Creamy white 'Sea Foam', a shrub rose that grows three feet tall, makes a showy display—its six-foot-long canes spill over and down a wall just as its name promises.

52 Hybrid musk and shrub roses are the most compatible roses for perennial borders. The spreading hybrid musks and shrub roses look more at home accompanied by perennials than the stiffer, more upright hybrid tea, floribunda, and grandiflora roses. I've learned from experience that hybrid teas, grandifloras, and floribundas don't bloom very well when crowded by companion plants, while the musks and shrubs are much more sociable, flowering profusely even when surrounded by cranesbills and bellflowers.

(53) Several of the floribunda roses are relaxed enough in their shapes to blend into borders. Most floribundas have smaller flowers that bloom in clusters. They look less formal than the hybrid teas and blend together well with perennials.

'Iceberg' is a choice floribunda for disease resistance and reliable flowering. It's a good mixer, with graceful double white flowers that are at home in any border. 'Escapade' grows happily in mixed borders too, its lavender-pink flowers compatible with blue-, pink-, white-, and light yellow-flowering perennials.

(54) For the earliest color and perfume, grow old roses. Even though most old roses bloom only once, they flower in spring, at least a month earlier than the reblooming modern hybrids. Their scent is often stronger and "rosier" than that of their contemporary cousins, and many flower in unique shades of rich purple-red and deep glowing pink, reminiscent of velvet and satin.

Traditionally, old roses have been defined as those introduced before 1867, but Roger Phillips and Martyn Rix, in *The Quest for the Rose*, extend the date to 1920 and include the early hybrid teas in the old rose group.

(55) Get a jump on the season with the earliest bloomers, both old and new. Once-blooming Father Hugo's rose (*Rosa hugonis*) leads the bloom parade in my garden. Single yellow roses open all along its ferny-leaved (but prickly-feeling) canes. Many of the stems are tinted red, adding to the plant's interest.

'Mary Queen of Scots', a medium-sized hybrid of the burnet rose (*Rosa spinosissima*) is also a season opener, with pink flowers. 'Maigold', a repeat-blooming Kordes rose introduced in 1953, can be grown as a large shrub or as a climber. The fragrant semidouble flowers are yellow with a hint of orange.

Rosa banksiae lutea makes a lovely thornless climber for warm-climate gardens, with profuse double yellow flowers. It blooms early enough to accompany wisteria, its clusters of small yellow roses a perfect contrast for wisteria's long lavender chains. Many gardeners in colder zones try growing this rose in the shelter of a warm wall, and some succeed, if only for a few years.

56 Rugosa roses are also among the first to open. Early to flower, the rugosas delight me with their sweetly scented large flowers and their shiny green, crinkled leaves that sparkle with health. Single pink *Rosa rugosa* and its white form, *Rosa rugosa alba*, start the color sequence, followed soon after by the hybrid forms—single pink 'Scabrosa', double white 'Blanc Double de Couvert', double magenta-pink 'Hansa', and pastel pink 'Delicata'.

Rugosas are resistant to black spot and powdery mildew, making them especially valuable in rainy climates, although they sometimes do suffer from rust.

57 Next to bloom are several of the species, or wild, roses and their closely related hybrids. Species are the original plants as found in nature before breeders began crossing and recrossing roses to develop hybrids. For the most part, their flowers are single, followed by ornamental hips. Mainly tall and wide spreading (8 to 10 feet across or more), they are useful for hedging and screening at the perimeter of the garden.

A few favorites: *Rosa macrantha* is pink in the bud, opening to a large, single light pink flower fading to white, with beautiful golden stamens at the center. This rose in bloom is sure to provoke "What is that?" from all viewers, as the flowers are big and plentiful and the fragrance is lovely. Red hips form later.

Rosa californica plena makes a glorious hedge or windbreak, with early-blooming semidouble pink flowers brushed with white, deliciously scented.

'Apothecary's Rose', also called 'Red Damask' (*Rosa gallica officinalis*) is early to bloom, with brilliant deep pink flowers. Tolerant of poor soil, asking for almost no care, and flowering for a good two months in early summer, 'Apothecary's Rose' stays under four feet tall, running happily underground to form a big colony. Every so often it sends up a few canes of its sport, 'Rosa Mundi' (*Rosa gallica versicolor*), with charming striped petals.

58 Choose at least a few of the old rose hybrids to bridge the gap between the earliest species and the summer-blooming modern roses. On the heels of the early species roses, the gallicas, damasks, albas, Bourbons, centifolias, and mosses create a riot of late spring and early summer color. Mainly flowering in shades of pink, crimson, and white, their colors are very compatible with each other.

(59) Make sure you have a few late-blooming roses to keep the color going into the fall. The musk rose (*Rosa moschata*), white and fragrant with a lovely sprinkling of golden stamens at the center, blooms in late summer and fall and can be trained to climb.

Rosa virginiana opens pink single flowers in July and continues into late summer. In the fall its normally shiny leaves turn golden and orange-red, and orange-red hips add to the show, decorating the bush long after the leaves have fallen. A handsome hedge of *R. virginiana* stands guard at Sissinghurst Castle, part of an autumnal display that includes *Euonymus* and *Viburnum* species.

Once-Blooming Old Roses

60 **Grow the larger species roses at the edge of woodland areas or at the back of borders.** Species, or wild, roses are the original forms as they occurred in nature—around 250 are known. Their beauty is simpler and quieter than that of their bigger, brighter hybrid progeny, with single flowers blooming once, for a month or two, followed by red, burgundy, or even blue-black fruits, known as hips.

The taller species roses grow 6 to 10 feet tall and equally wide and can be left nearly alone, with only occasional pruning to clean out dead wood or to remove old canes. Their colorful hips add value late in the season, when the garden is too often drab. Allowed to scramble and run, the shrubby species fit right into the more naturalized areas of the garden and provide good bird and wildlife habitat.

(61) Near hybrids of the species roses have been bred for bigger flowers and more prolific hips. *Rosa moyesii* 'Geranium' is a more compact form of its species parent, compact being a relative term–'Geranium' tops out at about eight feet. It has bright red single flowers and larger hips than the species. Its hips are a strong feature in the borders at Sissinghurst in autumn.

'Highdownensis', a seedling of *Rosa moyesii*, has single, bright pinkish red flowers and gorgeous red-orange hips. A specimen of *R. m.* 'Highdownensis' so laden with flagon-shaped hips that the branches drooped stopped me in my tracks one November at Van Dusen Botanic Gardens in Vancouver, B.C.

(62) I recommend *Rosa glauca*, **my favorite species rose, for its flowers, foliage, form, and hips.** "What's *that*?" most visitors inquire when they first spot *Rosa glauca*. When I tell them it's a rose they look at me with disbelief–understandably, because *Rosa glauca* has little resemblance to most roses. In early spring smoky burgundy leaves unfurl, followed by clusters of single pink flowers that stand out dramatically against the dark foliage. Wine-colored hips form as soon as the flowers fade. By late summer the hips have turned bright red-orange and remain on the leafless branches all winter.

My 10-year-old plant, six feet tall, with canes that arch gracefully eight feet wide, makes a dramatic focal point at the middle of a 30-foot-deep mixed border that screens the road from the house. *Rosa glauca* could also be grown at the back of a border along a property line or against a wall. It thrives in full sun or partial shade, coloring up more purplish in full sun and grayer green in shade.

63 **Grow gray-foliaged species roses to develop interesting color schemes.** *Rosa woodsii fendleri, R. fedtschenkoana, R. soulieana, R. villosa, R. 'Dupontii'* (technically a species hybrid), *R. beggeriana,* and *R. x alba* have gray-green leaves and white flowers. To emphasize the gray, add silvery herbs and perennials–artemisia, lavender, rue, gray santolina, lamb's ears, and cardoon. Plant white and pastel pink lilies, phloxes, and cranesbills to keep the color scheme cool.

If you prefer strong contrast, embellish with maroon-leaved plants such as *Sedum* 'Mohrchen', *Sedum maximum* 'Atropurpureum', 'Royal Purple' smoke tree, or *Euphorbia dulcis* 'Chameleon'. To contrast ice with fire, pair the gray-leaved roses with red-flowering perennials such as *Gaillardia* 'Burgundy' and *Crocosmia* 'Lucifer'.

64 Striking red thorns make *Rosa sericea pteracantha* a conversation piece. Ferny leaves, small white flowers, and glossy red pear-shaped hips make *Rosa sericea pteracantha* interesting enough, but the bright red winged thorns make it a novelty in a big enough border—it can shoot up 10 feet tall. Compellingly beautiful and cruel-looking, the flattened triangular red thorns have a translucent quality like stained glass. They are at their best on young canes, so cut it back hard each year (carefully!) to encourage new thorny branches. For the best effect, place this rose where the sun can come through it and illuminate the thorns. Perhaps this rose could be part of a "dangerous garden," together with globe thistle and barberry, rue and spurge, yucca and brambles, in which you could only garden armored with elbow-high gauntlets and long-handled loppers.

65 For outstanding fall color, plant *Rosa nitida*, *Rosa virginiana*, and *Rosa rugosa*. A native of North America, *Rosa nitida* has single deep pink flowers and glossy green leaves that turn deep red or purple in autumn, and decorative round red hips. It's low growing but suckers freely, making it most useful as a ground cover.

Rosa virginiana leafs out with bronze foliage that turns green in summer, then goes orange and yellow in the fall. Its flowers are cerise pink, followed by bright red hips that last well through the winter. Four to five feet tall, *R. virginiana* is suitable for a medium-sized hedge in the more natural parts of the garden.

The leaves of *Rosa rugosa* turn golden in fall, in striking contrast to the shiny red hips. Most rugosa roses stand at least five feet tall and look best at the back of the border or grown as informal hedges.

66 In wet places, plant *Rosa nitida* and *Rosa palustris*. *R. nitida* (described above) normally grows in bogs, wet thickets, and the edges of ponds, on acid soil. If your garden has similar habitats, *R. nitida* will adapt well. Similarly, *Rosa palustris*, the marsh rose, grows wild in swamps, marshes, and the edges of lakes. It flowers from late June into July, with single pink fragrant flowers showing golden stamens. In fall red hips form, and the leaves turn orange-red.

67 Grow once-blooming gallica roses for their fragrant early pink, mauve, and red-purple blooms. How can you distinguish a gallica from all the other categories of old roses? The green leaves are rough to touch, a bit sandpapery, and embossed with veins. The flowers are opulent and soul-satisfyingly scented. Gallicas bloom in a wide array of tints and shades—from palest blush to medium pink, bright pink, garnet, red-purple, and smoky purple, with no hint of orange-red.

Instead of thorns, gallicas have bristles and prickles along their stems. They're tolerant of poor soil, heavy clay, cold (hardy to zone 4), and neglect. I grow gallicas in the furthest reaches of the garden where they get the least attention, and they delight me every year with their showy display of exotic color.

68 'Tuscany', a popular gallica, is known as the Old Velvet Rose for good reason. 'Tuscany''s rich red-purple flowers open to show golden stamens. One whiff of 'Tuscany' and you will be sold. This is a great rose for the back of the border, blooming early enough in late spring to enjoy the company of early blue bellflowers (*Campanula latifolia*) and spikes of foxglove (*Digitalis purpurea*).

69 'Charles de Mills' is a classically beautiful gallica in form and color. A friend wins prizes at the rose show consistently with 'Charles de Mills'. Another throws a party every year when this rose is in bloom. The shape of the flower alone is enough to recommend it—especially large with a flattened face packed with petals that are folded into a pleasing quartered pattern. The outer petals encircle the inner petals in a way that frames the flower. As the rose ages its color changes from an early bright pink-purple to a darker red-purple, glorious in both stages.

70 For the darkest of all the gallicas, grow rich purple 'Cardinal de Richelieu'. If you're fond of purple and enjoy velvet, this is the rose for you. You won't find a reblooming rose with color this rich and sultry. Graham Stuart Thomas compared the color of 'Cardinal de Richelieu' to "the sumptuous bloom of a dark grape." Place this in the company of pink damask roses to add depth to the color scheme.

71 If your prefer pastels, pale pink 'Duchesse de Montebello' is heavenly. In full bloom this rose is an ethereal cloud of blush pink roses—I wouldn't be surprised to see angels lightly swinging from the canes.

'Duchesse de Montebello' is very fragrant and grows vigorously with little attention. Avoid planting strong yellow flowers near this rose–they will drown out its delicate beauty. White, blue, and deeper pink blooms are much more compatible.

72 **Enormous single pink flowers with white centers distinguish 'Complicata' from all other gallicas.** Once you see 'Complicata' you won't forget it, and you'll probably covet it enough to get one of your own. Its electric pink flowers first dazzled me in a New Zealand garden, where they glowed against a gray stone wall, and the memory lasted until I planted 'Complicata' at home, against a fence. Arching canes loaded with generous blooms spread six feet in all directions, making a bright pink accent visible from long distances. The name seems ironic, as the flowers couldn't be much simpler in shape and the plant couldn't be easier to grow. 'Complicata' will open your eyes to the beauty of single flowers.

73 **'Belle de Crecy' is a favorite gallica for its excellent fragrance and intriguing color changes.** Blossoms that open bright pink turn violet, then lavender, and eventually lavender-gray. 'Belle de Crecy''s four-foot canes are loaded down with flowers that open wide and flat, with reflexed petals that expose a green button eye at the center of each exquisite flower.

74 Damasks have the rich perfume you hope for from a rose. Damasks have gray-green leaves, super-fragrant flowers in shades of pink and white, and a vigorous growth pattern that results in arching shrubs. For the most part they work best at the back of the border where their flowers can be enjoyed at bloom time and their gray-green leaves serve as a low-key backdrop for later-flowering roses and perennials.

For the earliest damask flowers with rich perfume and long-lasting color, plant 'Ispahan'. Starting in spring, clusters of warm pink flowers weigh down the branches for a good two months, causing them to arch gracefully. Buds, partially opened flowers, and fully opened blooms appear on the same cluster, adding old-fashioned charm to the arrangement.

'Ispahan' is a vigorous grower, best suited for the larger garden. Its canes shoot skyward eight feet and more and eventually arch outward and down. During bloom time the ground below becomes as pink with petal fall as the shrub above, as more and more flowers bloom and wane.

75 **Treat yourself to luxurious fragrance for two months by planting 'La Ville de Bruxelles'.** Heavily scented and very double, rich pink flowers make 'La Ville de Bruxelles' a favorite in my garden. The branches spread wide, at least five feet in all directions, and the flowers bloom in clusters.

The older flowers turn papery, and the shrub's appearance is vastly improved by regular deadheading, well worth the effort because the fresh blooms are so big and showy. It's such a joy to work in the midst of 'La Ville de Bruxelles', enveloped in rose perfume, that I slow down and make the job last as long as possible. After the bloom period is over, I cut the lanky canes back by at least a third to tidy up the shape.

76 **If you're looking for an unusual damask rose, try 'Leda'.** It's always a surprise when 'Leda''s red buds explode into white flowers, and the bicolor effect of red buds coexisting with newly opened white flowers adds to 'Leda''s character. The petals keep a trace of red at their edges, as if the margins were painted with a fine brush, which accounts for 'Leda''s common name, painted damask.

(77) Everyone falls in love with 'Madame Hardy'—you will too. 'Madame Hardy' is adored for its large white flowers that start out cupped, open flat, and finally reflex to show a green button eye at the center. Blooming in clusters like other damasks, 'Madame Hardy' is usually classified a damask rose, but references attribute its elegant beauty to centifolia, alba, and Portland heritage. This rose was bred by Empress Josephine's gardener-in-chief at Malmaison and was named in honor of his wife.

(78) Here's how to tell an alba rose: the foliage is gray-green, the flowers are pink or white, and they grow so vigorously that many of them can be trained to climb trees. I have found the alba roses to be indestructible. Called "the white roses" because many are white and light pink, and "the tree roses" for their ability to climb trees, the albas are also tolerant of shade. They do require some room to spread, climb, or both, so give them space or they will gallop over the neighboring plants.

(79) 'Belle Amour', a fragrant semi-double pink alba rose, is a ter-

rific climber in tough places. I first saw 'Belle Amour' covering a pergola in Seattle and was smitten by the abundant color and fragrance. I planted mine at the base of an old comice pear tree and within four years it climbed to the top. Every June visitors ask me the name of the pink-blooming tree.

One spring I was horrified when a well-intentioned friend pruned 'Belle Amour' as if it were a hybrid tea (don't ever do that!). It took two years for the rose to bounce back and scramble up the pear tree. Very thorny canes help 'Belle Amour' climb, but fortunately little pruning is required except for removing dead wood and occasionally thinning out old canes.

80 The alba rose 'Königin von Dänemark' ('Queen of Denmark') makes a four-to-five-foot-tall shrub that colonizes well. Beloved for its shapely pink roses that open flat and are quartered with a green button eye, 'Königin von Dänemark' stays shrubby, running moderately to form a thicket of gray-green foliage. Because it can take sun or shade, I've planted mine to make a good transition where a sunny bed becomes shady.

81 'Madame Plantier' can be trained to climb or allowed to grow

as a spreading shrub. Outstanding fragrance and double white flowers comparable to 'Madame Hardy' for their loveliness cover 'Madame Plantier''s arching branches for two months. The pink buds, which continue to hold color as the white flowers open, add delightful detail. If there is ample room this rose may be allowed to roam and scramble—mine travels a good 10 feet, swelling into an ocean of white flowers in June. If space is short, train 'Madame Plantier' up an arbor or onto a trellis.

82 Think of the cabbage roses on chintz sofas, and you will easily picture centifolias. Captured for eternity by Dutch and Flemish painters, and often reproduced on fabric and wallpaper, thc cabbage roses are among the most opulent and fragrant roses. Although the flowers are sumptuous, often the lanky canes are lax and benefit from the support of a fence or wall. Most grow at least six feet tall and expand equally wide. (A centifolia I saw growing in a New Zealand garden was so dense it actually had a bird's nest tucked into the branches!)

'Fantin-Latour' is the centifolia I've seen most often in large gardens, usually blooming forward of a fence. The blowsy light pink flowers open cupped, and eventually the outer petals reflex backward, adding grace. 'Paul Ricault' is also a very popular centifolia, with flat-faced, deep pink flowers that are beautifully quartered and a strong old-rose fragrance.

83 If your garden is small, enjoy the miniature centifolias. 'Petite de Hollande' is a more compact form of centifolia, growing three to four feet tall, with the same beautifully shaped flowers as its taller relatives. The pink petals are pastel toward the margins and a deeper shade of rose pink toward the center of the flower, as if to draw you into its heart.

'De Meaux' is also considered a miniature centifolia, but the pink flowers are tighter, in more of a pompom shape, and opening flat. A white form, 'White de Meaux', has pink-centered white flowers.

Any of the miniature centifolias may be grown in smaller gardens or used toward the front of big borders in larger gardens.

84 Grow at least one moss rose in your garden, for the unique texture and good perfume. Moss roses are sports, or mutations, of the centifolia roses, distinguished by a fuzzy-looking mosslike covering on their buds and stems. Many of my students ask, "Are those aphids?" At first glance, the resemblance is unfortunate. But once you know the little green bumps are a resinous mossy material and not bugs, they take on a much more charming quality. Buds appear to be cozily nestled in a soft surround of velvety, bright green moss that you can't help but touch, just the way you have to pat lamb's ears.

85 **Of all the mosses, my favorite (so far) is 'William Lobb'.** When exotic deep wine, nearly purple, and very double flowers open, there's no doubt that this is a thrilling rose. Its delightful fragrance is typical of the moss roses. 'William Lobb' has wide-spreading, straggly canes and is best grown at the back of the border, where its sensational flowers can hover over shorter roses and perennials. After it's finished blooming I cut back the bristly canes by at least one-third their length, and new growth proceeds to thicken up the bush.

86 **Although most moss roses bloom only once, 'Mrs. William Paul', 'Salet', and 'Alfred de Dalmas' ('Mousseline') repeat.** The repeat-blooming mosses are compact shrubs, deserving a place in the smaller garden. 'Mrs. William Paul' is the brightest of these, pink with red shading, while 'Salet' is medium pink. 'Alfred de Dalmas', also known as 'Mousseline' (for its likeness to fine French muslin) blushes ethereal pink-tinted ivory, and is also the least mossy of the three.

87 Prune once-blooming roses after flowering, in July. When the flowers are spent, cut the flowering stems back to a place on the cane that's starting to generate a new branch. I prune lanky canes back by about one-third their length to shape the shrub. This is also a good time to remove some of the older, woody canes back to the base of an older bush. This will generate fresh new growth from the ground level.

Reblooming Old Roses

88 **Be sure to deadhead reblooming roses after each flowering period.** Both for cosmetic reasons and to encourage further bloom, cut back the flowering branches as soon as the blooms are spent. Look for a swelling along the cane that points outward, and make your cut just above that place to encourage the new shoots to grow toward the outside of the plant.

If the spent flowering shoots are on the lanky side, use this opportunity to cut the canes back by one-third or so to improve the shape of the bush. This is also a good time to remove twiggy shoots along the inside of the canes and any wood that has died back (it will look brown and lifeless).

(89) **China roses are especially valuable for warm climates.** Hardy in zones 7–10, the China roses do best in the South and California. They can be grown in cooler climates with protection of a wall or increased warmth from a raised bed, or on their own roots with a winter mulch, with the understanding that they may die back in a cold winter and return from below ground.

Chinas are relatively airy shrubs with pointed leaves and silky flowers. When they were introduced to the West from China some two hundred years ago, they were the first to contribute their invaluable reblooming ability to the gene pool. Without China roses, hybrid teas, floribundas, and all the reblooming roses we treasure would probably never have arisen.

(90) **'Mutabilis' and its seedling 'Mateo's Silk Butterflies' are two of the most unusual and beautiful China roses.** Single flowers that open soft yellow and deepen to pink and then red are poised so gracefully on the branches that 'Mutabilis' is often known as the "butterfly rose." The unlikely mix of red, pink, and yellow on the same shrub is enchanting—I can stare at it forever.

'Mateo's Silk Butterflies' is a seedling of 'Mutabilis' bred by Kleine Lettunich of Corralitos, California. Similar to

'Mutabilis', it's covered with a blend of pink, yellow, and red flowers from spring until fall. An added advantage is its drought resistance.

91 **Hybrid perpetual roses arose in the 19th century, and we'd probably still be growing them if the hybrid teas hadn't been introduced starting in 1867.** The first hybrid perpetual was probably a cross between a reblooming China rose and a once-blooming old rose, but eventually Noisettes, Chinas, Bourbons, and Portlands all went into the soup. Many new varieties were introduced each year—more than three thousand (!) hybrid perpetuals existed at one time—a lot like the flood of hybrid teas and floribundas that poured forth in the 20th century.

It's hard to generalize about hybrid perpetuals because the plants vary a great deal. Most have big, fragrant flowers on blowsy bushes, all rebloom, and the colors are maroon, purple, pink, crimson, white, and stripes of these colors.

92 **For an impenetrable hedge that is also ornamental and fragrant, you can't beat *Rosa rugosa*, the sea tomato rose, and its hybrids.** Rugosa roses offer shiny green leaves that look embossed; reblooming flowers in white, pink, and red; and large red fruit in the fall. Their scent is often spicy-sweet, hinting of cloves. The single-flowered rugosas open wide to display golden stamens, and heavy black bumblebees with full saddlebags of pollen are frequent visitors.

Most rugosas grow at least six feet tall, ideal for hedging, and their wicked thorns can be an advantage where you wish to discourage intruders. Immune to mildew and black spot, they are occasionally attacked by rust.

93 **Gorgeous double purplish pink flowers that smell delicious and whopper hips make the hybrid rugosa 'Hansa' outstanding.** 'Hansa' stands six feet tall, loaded with fragrant flowers in spring. The round hips that follow in midsummer and fall are so shiny they look like they've been lacquered. 'Hansa' gets more attention from visitors than any other rugosa rose.

94 **For a white garden, it's hard to outdo the hybrid rugosa 'Blanc Double de Couvert'.** This is one of the earliest roses to flower and one of the sweetest smelling. The new buds are blush pink, opening to semidouble white flowers that are delicate and translucent, like oriental poppies. 'Blanc

Double de Couvert' runs underground to form a moderate-sized colony, and stands about five feet tall.

95 **When it comes to deadheading reblooming rugosas that also set hips, strike a compromise so that you can have both flowers and fruit.** I deadhead the front half of the bush to keep the blooms going and let the back half set hips for the birds and for making jelly.

96 **If you have a small garden, try the more compact hybrid rugosa 'Fru Dagmar Hastrup'.** Topping out at about four feet tall and spreading nearly as wide, 'Fru Dagmar Hastrup' has very generous single pink flowers that continue to bloom at the same time that the hips are forming, so that flowers and hips coincide delightfully on the same shrub.

97 **Fast growing and running rapidly underground, 'Scabrosa' is a great rose where you need quick cover.** Big single pink flowers that draw the bees and bright green shiny leaves that look good enough to eat made me choose 'Scabrosa' in the first place. But when I saw how quickly the plant filled out and spread, I dug out runners and planted them elsewhere in the garden where I needed extra thickness. 'Scabrosa' is excellent as part of an informal hedge, standing an ultimate six feet tall. It sets huge red hips for fall.

98 **For cold climates, 'Therese Bugnet' is about the toughest rugosa, hardy to zone 2.** Even though 'Therese Bugnet' looks much more like a hybrid than a species, with old-fashioned, ruffled flowers, this rose has all the hardiness of the toughest wild roses. Burgundy tints along the stems create color echoes with the lavender-pink blossoms. The flowers and leaves are medium sized, in good proportion to each other.

99 **Bourbon roses are known for their opulent cupped flowers and very strong scent.** Bourbons start blooming with the old roses and rebloom well during the summer and fall. Many are vigorous enough to grow as climbers, and their long flexible canes make them easy to train on fences and walls.

Grow 'Zephirine Drouhin', a most unusual Bourbon, as a large brilliant shrub, or enjoy it climbing up a trellis. Bright pink flowers, electric enough to draw your attention from a distance, open wide for maximum color and a glimpse of golden stamens. You must always pause to take a whiff of the lovely fragrance. Left alone, it makes an arching shrub that spreads wide. The smooth, thornless canes and stems are easy to train on a trellis or arbor. Unfortunately 'Zephirine Drouhin' is very susceptible to mildew and black spot, which mar the new foliage, especially in rainy climates. Nevertheless, the later leaves emerge bright green and smooth, flattering the bright pink flowers.

(100) For fun and fragrance, try the striped Bourbon 'Honorine de Brabant'. Sweet-smelling cupped flowers of pale pink striped with violet bloom heavily in spring and continue all summer long. This Bourbon is six feet tall and nearly as wide, standing upright rather than arching. In my garden, it's never suffered from black spot or mildew and has much lusher foliage than 'Variegata di Bologna', another striped Bourbon so plagued by black spot that I dug it out.

'Honorine de Brabant' is a perfect trellis for my favorite purple clematis, 'Etoile Violette', which snakes through it and continues romping through 'Vanity', a tall hybrid musk.

(101) Big, rich purplish pink flowers and a heady perfume make 'Ma-

dame Isaac Pereire' one of the showiest Bourbons. One glimpse of the voluptuous flowers rarely fails to kindle a desire to own this rose. The very large and vibrant flowers are cupped at first and open to a quartered pattern. This is a must-have rose if you appreciate strong fragrance. The early leaves often suffer from black spot, so preventive spraying is recommended, but even without spraying, the rebloom is good and the later leaves are healthy.

Left as a shrub, 'Madame Isaac Pereire' spreads a good eight feet wide, and the pliable arching canes lend well to training on a wall or fence.

(102) 'La Reine Victoria' offers shapely pink flowers on a medium-sized shrub. The rounded flowers hold their graceful gobletlike form, standing upright against the light green leaves. A slender shrub that fits well into the smaller garden, 'La Reine Victoria' possesses a delicate beauty that I never tire of.

(103) Hybrid musks are an invaluable group of reblooming roses that are characterized by clusters of small flowers, good fragrance, and excellent repeat bloom. This is by far my favorite group of roses, for along with the rugosas and species, they are extremely healthy and undemanding. They've adapted well to the wet climate here in the Pacific Northwest and to my soil, which, although amended continually with compost, is still clay based.

Many of the hybrid musks make gracefully wide-spreading shrubs that are compatible with perennials in mixed borders. The large clusters of small flowers have an old-fashioned charm, yet bloom continuously as well or better than many of the modern roses. Hybrid musks grow well in full sun or partial shade.

(104) Where there's plenty of room, hybrid musk 'Vanity' is a magnificent rose. 'Vanity' deserves its name. Clusters of large single flowers of a pink so brilliant that it's close to magenta are carried at the very tips of the high-reaching canes. The bush grows seven to eight feet tall and spreads even wider, with enough space between the branches for delphinium or speedwell to rocket through the openings. 'Vanity' sets large hips, but I usually don't get to enjoy them—I'm too intent on deadheading the spent flowers to encourage the next cycle of bloom. This rose starts blooming early and continues very late into the fall, when the fragrance is strongest and most appreciated.

(105) **For the best display of continuous pink flowers, plant 'Lavender Lassie'.** Gracefully arching branches loaded with clusters of pink flowers make 'Lavender Lassie' a delightfully informal shrub. The color is a refreshing cool pink tinted with a light suggestion of lavender. This hybrid musk rose climbs beautifully onto an arch or trellis—the canes are long and flexible—and the flowers are continuous.

(106) **Where you want a bright accent that's hardly ever out of bloom, it's hard to surpass 'Mozart'.** Huge clusters of reddish pink flowers, each with a white eye at the center, turn this hybrid musk into a beacon. I enjoy it from my office window, more than 50 feet away from the mixed border where 'Mozart' reigns. Starting in May, this rose is smothered in bright flowers, and three later strong flushes of bloom during the summer and fall are excellent too.

It takes me about an hour to deadhead 'Mozart', so you can imagine how many flowers it produces. I figure that one hour's work a few times a year is worth the months of pleasure that 'Mozart' gives me. After the last bloom period the spent flowers form small orange hips. My six-year-old shrub is about five feet tall and at least eight feet across.

(107) **Use the taller hybrid musks as backdrop shrubs.** 'Kathleen', with clusters of pale pink flowers resembling apple blossoms, and 'Buff Beauty', an unusual shade of soft yellow with a hint of orange, both grow tall enough for the back of a border, or they may be trained as short climbers. I've seen each of these grown very nicely against the wall of a house in partial shade.

Several of the pale-tinted hybrid musks actually do better in shade than in sun. Pastel pink 'Ballerina', white 'Prosperity', and white 'Sally Holmes' tend to fade very quickly in bright sunlight. The flowers last a lot longer in dappled shade and show up very nicely there too, illuminating the darker beds and borders.

'Moonlight', a white hybrid musk, is an excellent shrub or climber for shade. I accidentally planted 'Moonlight' in a bed that was shadier than I knew and discovered that it didn't mind at all. The clusters of semidouble flowers with beautiful golden stamens bloomed vigorously on long pliable canes. Not only that, but it began to climb a pear tree all on its own.

Modern
Roses

108 The best way to grow healthy modern roses is by themselves, in raised beds. Modern roses were bred to produce bigger and showier flowers in a wide range of colors. The size, color, and form of the flower itself became the focus, and very little attention was paid to the shape of the rosebush as a landscape plant. The point was to have a gorgeous flower to cut for bouquets and to exhibit in competitive rose shows.

Unfortunately, these big showy flowers bloom on stiff-looking canes—the upright form of a hybrid tea or grandiflora rosebush is hard to combine visually with billowing perennials. And even if looks are not a concern, modern roses don't bloom well in the company of other plants—they like their own bed with rich, well-draining soil. In my opinion, the best way to grow roses intended for cutting and showing is in a cutting garden—that way you can enjoy their beauty in a vase and not fret about how to incorporate them into your garden design.

109 **Prune modern roses (hybrid teas, floribundas, grandifloras, polyanthas, and miniature roses) every spring to generate new flowering canes. Start by removing the dead wood.** To produce a healthy bush that flowers well, cut all the brown, woody dead canes all the way down to their origin (don't leave stubs) with long-handled loppers or a small pruning saw. The exception to this rule is if there are very few canes on the bush, and an old brown cane has large green healthy canes sprouting from it. Leave it alone, and prune the green canes the same way you would prune any other healthy canes.

110 **Next, eliminate crossing branches and twiggy growth.** Two crossing canes will rub against each other and also produce a congested bush vulnerable to mildew, black spot, and aphids. Remove the cane pointing toward the center of the plant and leave the one that is more easily pruned to face out in order to produce a more open, airy bush. Then note the healthiest five to seven canes—they will be green and sturdy. Leave these on the plant and remove the rest, which may be spindly or spotted or too close together. Cut off any weak twiggy growth along the canes.

111 **Prune the remaining canes just above a dormant bud that faces the outside of the bush.** Finally, cut the healthy canes down to about two feet tall, making your cut about one-fourth inch above a node that faces the outside of the plant. (Nodes are those faint horizontal lines or swellings that appear all along the rose canes.) This will force the plant to sprout new wood, which will bear this year's flowers.

Although the ideal rosebush, after pruning, has anywhere from five to seven smooth green canes cut back to two feet tall, often, in order to have a balanced shape, you will end up with six or eight halfway-decent canes or only three canes because that's all there are. Relax—the rose will grow and branch out as the season progresses. Just do the best you can with the plant as it is.

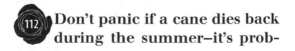**112** **Don't panic if a cane dies back during the summer—it's prob-**

ably not your fault—just cut it out. I've been alarmed when suddenly a cane that bore flowers turns brownish or pale green and sickly looking. Often this is just the long-term effect of winter damage that occurred earlier but took awhile to kick in. An injured cane may produce a few blooms at first, like a dying swan's song, and then go downhill. Prune the cane down to the ground, and you'll be rewarded by new shoots originating from the base of the plant.

(113) Get the best qualities of both the old and new roses by growing English roses. David Austin backcrossed old roses with hybrid teas and floribundas to produce shrubs that bloom throughout the summer (with the exception of 'Constance Spry' and 'Chianti', which only bloom once), yet also retain the colors, scent, and shapes of the old roses. These hybrids allow you to enjoy the cupped, flattened, and quartered shapes of the old roses and their delicate tints and deep rich colors and also get the repeat bloom of the modern roses.

Because Austin's crosses involved so many classifications of roses, these hybrids are as diverse as their ancestors and have widely differing heights, habits, and vigor. I'll describe some of the best to give you a sampler.

114 Heady perfume and nonstop flowering make 'Gertrude Jekyll', one of David Austin's English roses, a standout. 'Gertrude Jekyll' blooms all summer and fall with double rich pink flowers. The central petals stay deep pink while the outer petals grow paler, giving the flower extra depth. Freshly opened flowers have a quartered pattern that reminds me of old roses; as the flowers open fully, golden stamens sparkle at the center. I would grow this rose for its scent alone–marvelously sweet and rosy.

A tall shrub, 'Gertrude Jekyll' can also be trained to climb a trellis or a wall. If you wish to keep this rose bushy, prune it down to three or four feet in spring and cut back lanky canes during the growing season. Just remember to wear your leather gloves–it's as thorny as it's gorgeous!

115 Tall and stately with bewitching grace, 'English Elegance' deserves a place in every garden. Is it pink, peach, or salmon? All of the above, and very hard to pin down. The new flowers of 'English Elegance' open salmon-pink and pale to a soft peach. I love this rose against the burgundy foliage of purple-leaved loosestrife (*Lysimachia ciliata* 'Atropurpurea').

The inner petals twist in a beguiling way, and the flowers nod gracefully on arching canes. Beautiful in arrangements, the large blooms have a charming silhouette. A pleasing fragrance accompanies these unique flowers.

116 **In smaller gardens, save room for 'The Countryman'.** A favorite English rose for its gracefully arching canes—I let it drape over a carpet of gray-leaved cottage pinks. 'The Countryman' bears large and profuse double pink flowers with the flattened faces of old roses, and it has a refreshing fragrance, a blend of sweet and fruity. Three to four feet tall and five feet wide, 'The Countryman' is well worth the space it occupies.

117 **'Othello' is as showy in a bouquet as in the garden.** Jumbo, very double flowers of deep pinkish red are marvelous for cutting, with a satisfying fragrance. Healthy green leaves support the flowers.

118 **If you appreciate ethereal beauty, plant 'Sharifa Asma'.** Imagine pale pink chiffon or whipping cream tinted pastel pink and you'll get the picture. Delicate in color yet powerfully fragrant, 'Sharifa Asma' is a most romantic English rose, with large, breathtakingly beautiful flowers. To see it is to want it.

(119) Several of the taller English roses are suitable for climbing and useful as backdrop screening, especially in warmer climates. I've seen 'Graham Stuart Thomas', a very well liked double yellow English rose, climbing an arbor in New Zealand, and double pink 'Gertrude Jekyll' reaching up a gazebo in Oregon. 'Hero', 'Red Coat', and 'Heritage' are also in this group of tall English roses.

(120) Find a place for 'Parkdirektor Riggers'—it's a knock-your-socks-off-gorgeous red shrub or climber. I admired 'Parkdirektor Riggers' many times in other gardens before I took the leap and introduced a deep red rose to my largely pink rose collection. Like many such steps, now I think "Why didn't I do it sooner?!" Velvety red semidouble flowers that are ruffled at the edges glow against lustrous dark green leaves that remain impeccable without any spraying. This rose can be placed as a vigorous large shrub or trained to climb.

'Parkdirektor Riggers' was introduced by the firm of Kordes Sohne in 1957, and in my opinion, any rose introduced by Kordes will glow with health—'Erfurt' and 'Dortmund' head my list. The story is told that the younger Wilhelm Kordes (son of the nursery's founder, Wilhelm Senior) was held captive on the Isle of Man during World War I, spent his time studying everything in print about rose breeding, and applied his knowledge after the war was over.

Climbing
Roses

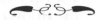

121 **For practical purposes, there are three kinds of climbing roses to consider: ramblers, large-flowered climbers, and vigorous shrubs.** Rambling roses are the most flexible climbers, with long pliable canes and showy clusters of flowers. Many are fragrant, and most bloom only once in spring and early summer, for a month or two. Most multiflora and sempervirens ramblers have small flowers, while most of the wichuraiana and noisette ramblers have larger blooms. Ramblers are easy to train up trees and onto fences, walls, and arbors. Most require very little pruning.

Large-flowered climbers generally have bigger flowers than ramblers and canes that are stiffer and often thornier. Most, but not all, rebloom, and some are fragrant. They're best suited for training and tying onto a flat surface such as a wall, pillar, or fence–their canes don't flex easily, and it's difficult to bend them over an arch. There are also a large number of tall shrub, hybrid musk, and Bourbon roses that may be trained to climb–most of these are as flexible as the ramblers.

(122) Even though once-blooming ramblers flower for a shorter period of time than reblooming climbers, their color impact is often stronger. Ramblers are like concentrated fireworks–their flowers burst forth all at once in a dazzling display that lasts anywhere from three weeks to two months. To me, this strong surge of color is more worthwhile than a few flowers here and there scattered over a period of several months. When you consider that many of the once-blooming ramblers flower way ahead of the reblooming climbers, you can more easily forgive their limited season.

Reblooming climbers vary in the amount of color they provide. Some bloom heavily in spring, then sporadically in summer and fall, while others bloom more continuously through the season.

123 Prune once-blooming ramblers lightly in the summer after they're finished blooming and in the spring if you need to limit the number of canes so that the plant fits on the structure without overwhelming it. After bloom period, trim the stems back about six inches below the spent flowers. You may want to remove some canes at this time, as ramblers tend to shoot every which way, and depending on the size of your structure, some thinning may be useful to keep the rambler from looking like a huge jumble.

In the spring, the same is true. Pruning is done mainly to remove the excess growth. Ramblers have a tendency to take over the world, and your fence or trellis very likely has a fixed surface. Be assertive and don't be afraid to trim out extra canes clear to the ground–the rose will take it with grace, just like a stylish haircut.

124 The rambler 'Veilchenblau' blooms once, but I look forward to those glorious two months every year. Clusters of small semidouble purple flowers enlivened by streaks of white cover the smooth, nearly thornless canes. A delightful fruity scent wafts through the garden beckoning you to come closer and take another whiff.

'Veilchenblau' starts flowering early in spring and continues into summer.

It's happiest in partial shade and makes a glorious garland of purple when trained to the top of a fence. This rambler is robust enough to cover the face of a house, if you send it up a trellis or thread it through a wire grid. It's also strong enough to scramble into a tree and drape down, showering cascades of purple flowers from the branches overhead. One small stem that I cut to keep nearby as I write this carries 45 adorable flowers, so imagine the display from hundreds of stems that cover the canes.

(125) To train a rose up a tree, plant it on the sunny side. It's hard enough for a rose to compete with thick tree roots and dry soil. Give it a fighting chance by finding the sunniest location, as far from the trunk as possible. Dig a big hole and add good soil and plenty of compost at the bottom. Train the rose toward the lower branches with sturdy rope, and water it well on a regular basis.

When a tree dies, consider saving it as a rose trellis instead of taking it down. I saw some fine examples of climbing roses growing this way in New Zealand. You'll have to exercise patience, since it will take a few years for the rose to cover the tree skeleton, but you'll find it's worth waiting when the project is accomplished.

Numerous ramblers are good tree climbers: 'Seagull', 'Kiftsgate', 'Paul's Himalayan Musk', 'Bobbie James', 'Wedding Day', 'Rambling Rector', and 'Alberic Barbier' are a few of the most popular.

126 **When training a rose on a wall or trellis, pull canes horizontally, or at least at an angle.** Then tie them loosely to the trellis with a soft material such as jute, twine, or plastic nursery tape (stay away from wire or twisters with wire inside that can cut into the branches). This encourages the cane to break new flowering shoots all along its length, forming many more flowers than if it were shooting straight up in the air, where it would have a few lonely flowers blooming way up at the top of the branch, hard to see and impossible to smell.

127 **Choose a shorter climbing rose that is flexible for a pillar, post, or obelisk, and wind the canes spirally around the support.** This is as close as you can get to pulling the canes horizontally to force more flowering shoots into growth. You may have to tie the canes lightly to the support with jute to keep them from coming loose in the wind.

The following short climbers with pliable canes are very suitable for pillars: red 'Altissimo', red 'Dortmund', or bright pink 'Zephirine Drouhin'; red 'Gruss an Teplitz'; and white 'Climbing Iceberg'.

128 'New Dawn' is one of the most popular climbers for cold climates. Shiny foliage and heavy flowering are two qualities that convinced me to grow 'New Dawn' over a big arbor. The double, soft pink flowers are lightly fragrant and bloom most heavily in late spring, with occasional light flushes during the summer. This is a vigorous rose that will quickly cover an eyesore or a pergola, turning it into a pastel paradise. Equally beautiful is the ground beneath 'New Dawn', covered with pink petals that have floated to earth.

129 If you like ruffles, try the red climber 'Dortmund'. Large, brilliant red five-petaled flowers with white bullseyes that make them even more vibrant bloom in great clusters. Henry Mitchell likens it to bougainvillea, and those of us in climates too cold for bougainvillea can at least have the thrill of 'Dortmund'. This relatively short climber is suitable for a post, pillar, or garden arch.

130 Notice the way that some climb ing roses nod, adding grace.
Some of the most charming climbers have weak necks, so that the roses droop invitingly toward us. 'Spanish Beauty', also known as 'Madame Gregoire Staechelin', has this delightful effect of cascading towards you. The glowing pink flowers are ruffled on the edges and fragrant. Even though it blooms only once and is susceptible to rust in very wet climates, to see 'Spanish Beauty' is to covet it.

'Madame Alfred Carriere' is a white noisette climber that droops attractively. The fragrant flowers repeat well and are even tolerant of partial shade.

131 Many shrub, hybrid musk, and Bourbon roses can be trained to climb. With a structure to clamber over and a little encouragement in the form of prodding and tying, tall bushy roses grow upward into climbers instead of arching sideways into large shrubs. Several of David Austin's English shrub roses grow vigorously enough to train as climbers, especially in warm climates. Yellow 'Graham Stuart Thomas', pink 'Heritage', deep pink 'Gertrude Jekyll', and pink 'Constance Spry' send up long enough canes to train up a trellis very nicely.

The same holds for the more robust hybrid musks, such as pink 'Lavender

Lassie' and delicate apple-blossom pink 'Kathleen', and the strapping Bourbons, say vivid pink 'Zephirine Drouhin', light pink 'Kathleen Harrop', and reddish pink 'Madame Isaac Pereire'.

Many of the new shrub roses qualify too. 'New Face' covers a huge section of a gridded fence between my garden and my neighbor's, brightening it with clusters of single pink flowers flushed with yellow. Orange-pink 'Westerland', yellow 'Lichtkonigin Lucia', white 'Pleine de Grace', and red 'Scharlachglut' ('Scarlet Fire') are just a few of the shrub roses capable of scaling a wall or fence.

132 **Use an existing woody shrub or hedge to train a climber.** In a friend's garden, several established lilacs edging a driveway act as a trellis for 'Bobbie James', a fragrant rambler with clusters of large semidouble flowers that open to show golden stamens.

133 **Be sure to give newly planted climbers plenty of water, especially when planted near a wall or next to an established tree or shrub.** Roses trained to climb a house wall or even a wall enclosing the garden are vulnerable to drying out—the roots may be under the eaves or out of the reach

of rain beneath a tree or shrub canopy.
Make sure to water these climbers thoroughly and regularly, especially in the
first year or so.

Complementary Companions

134 **Double your vertical color by combining climbing roses with clematis.** Whether your climbing rose blooms once or reblooms, it will look even better with clematis flowers for company.

When it comes to rambling roses that need very little pruning, consider pairing them with clematis that also need little pruning—the *alpina, macropetala,* and *montana* species and hybrids.

Reblooming roses that need late winter pruning are best paired with those that bloom in summer and need pruning all the way down to the ground in late winter—the *jackmanii, viticella,* and *texensis* species and hybrids. That way you can clean up the clematis debris right around the same time as you prune your roses.

135 **For the best results, give your climbing rose a few years to establish itself before you train a clematis up its canes.** It takes a climbing rose three years to really get going and fling itself up a structure. Wait until it has some height before you send a vine after it or the clematis will be waving around in midair looking for a foothold. This is especially true if you're growing own-root roses, which start off not much bigger than a cutting.

Dig a generous hole for the clematis, and amend the soil with plenty of compost and a sprinkling of lime. Bury the vine a little deeper than it sits in its container, just as if you were planting a tomato—this helps prevent fungal diseases. Protect your new clematis by surrounding the base with old shingles or a few rocks to keep animals and human feet away from the vulnerable lower stems—if those are broken, your plant can go into decline. Train it up the rose canes (or up a trellis) by hand at first—clematis always seem to want to sprawl on the ground or tangle themselves up in a big wad.

136 **Purple, blue, and blue-violet clematis make wonderful part-**

ners for climbing roses. Purple clematis will pair well with just about any color rose. Try *Clematis* 'Etoile Violette', 'Gypsy Queen', or 'Polish Spirit' with the following climbers for striking color duets: yellow 'Golden Showers', deep pink 'Bantry Bay', or velvety red 'Don Juan'. Add some purple perennials at the base to pull it all together–clustered bellflower (*Campanula glomerata*) or false indigo (*Baptisia australis*), for example.

Blue and blue-violet clematis are also easygoing partners, especially 'Perle d'Azur', with medium-sized, very graceful and profuse flowers and 'Ramona' and 'Elsa Spaeth', with larger, showy blue flowers. Blue clematis are lovely in contrast with yellow, peach, and pink climbing roses. Add blue and blue-violet speedwells (*Veronica spicata*) and asters (*Aster x frikartii* 'Monch') for a finishing touch.

(137) **Pair pink, deep pink, and burgundy-colored clematis with climbing roses in related hues.** I've seen the beautiful deep pink *Clematis* 'Julia Correvon' combined with the bright pink reblooming Bourbon climber 'Zephirine Drouhin' and with the once-blooming Spanish Beauty rose 'Madame Gregoire Staechelin'. Deep wine-colored *Clematis* 'Niobe' pairs just as beautifully with either of these roses.

138 **Clematis and shrub roses are terrific partners.** 'Westerland', a scintillating shrub rose that blends shades of orange and peach in a most appealing way, and purple clematis 'Etoile Violette' are a great team, both being vigorous growers in complementary colors. Hot pink roses such as 'Cerise Bouquet' (a shrub rose) and 'Vanity' (a hybrid musk) pair up well with blue 'Perle d'Azur' clematis.

139 **Combine once-blooming species roses with clematis that bloom in summer or fall for late flowers that enhance the rose hips.** Let any of the white, late-flowering clematis travel up the base of a species rose that produces fall hips, and you will have a delightful red and white combination. *Clematis* 'Huldine', *C. viticella* 'Alba Luxurians', and *C. maximowicziana* are all good candidates for growing up *Rosa glauca*, *Rosa rugosa* 'Hansa', or any of the fruiting *Rosa moyesii* hybrids–'Sealing Wax', 'Geranium', or 'Highdownensis'.

140 **For a late-summer surprise, add yellow *Clematis tangutica* at the base of a reblooming rose.** The pendant golden bells of *Clematis tangutica* add a delightful touch to a trellis filled with reblooming roses in warm tones–

'Joseph's Coat', a blended rose of orange, red, and yellow, red 'Don Juan', or red 'Dublin Bay'.

141 **Follow a once-blooming rambler with a late-blooming clematis for a sequence of color on the same arbor.** Get more mileage from your structures and extend garden color into late summer by starting out with an early-flowering rose and continuing with a summer or fall-blooming clematis. 'Rambling Rector' can provide your early show with an abundance of fragrant white flowers, and *Clematis* 'Hagley Hybrid', with pinkish mauve flowers, can carry the color into late summer.

Purple lovers can start off the season with the luscious rambler 'Bleu Magenta' and continue it with *Clematis* 'Purpurea Plena Elegans', with double flowers in a color between purple and violet that's difficult to coordinate with roses and best by itself or with a creamy white rose.

142 **Plant shrubby clematis at the base of roses to make a froth of color that enhances the roses.** A small group of clematis don't climb and twine, but billow and lean (or flop, if there's nothing to lean on!) and need a sturdy plant to wander through. Roses are the perfect host for this casual relationship.

Clematis x durandii, with large deep blue flowers, makes a lovely accompaniment to deep pink 'Betty Prior', a floribunda, or peachy yellow 'Buff Beauty', a tall hybrid musk. *Clematis recta,* with hundreds of tiny white flowers, is as dainty as baby's breath at the base of the pink-flowering hybrid musk 'Lavender Lassie'.

143 **Add vertical spikes of color to rose beds by planting foxgloves (*Digitalis purpurea*), purple toadflax (*Linaria purpurea*), and speedwell (*Veronica spicata*).** Quite by accident foxgloves seeded in between the rugosa roses that screened my neighbor's yard, and purple toadflax traveled from the compost pile to a border of nearby shrub roses. Blue speedwell seeded down near the bright pink Bourbon rose 'Madame Isaac Pereire' and in front of a pink hybrid musk, 'Lavender Lassie'. These happy accidents taught me the value of vertical flower spikes punctuating the rounded rosebushes. Once you've planted a few of any of these perennials, they'll self-sow more than you can guess, so deadhead most of the spent flowers to prevent a jungle, or yank out excess seedlings mercilessly.

144 **Common as cabbages, lady's mantle (*Alchemilla mollis*) and**

lamb's ears (*Stachys lanata*) are sturdy edging plants for rose borders. Keep the weeds down around roses by planting with these old-fashioned perennials. Lady's mantle unfurls beautiful lobed leaves that catch the morning dew and offers sprays of yellow flowers that billow for months and make excellent filler for bouquets. Deadhead these flowers after they're spent to avoid a crop of lady's mantle.

Lamb's ears' furry leaves appeal to children and the child in all of us. The strange flower spikes, also furry, with tiny purple blooms tucked in the wool, tend to flop soon after opening, making tidy gardeners prefer the sterile form, 'Silver Carpet'. 'Big Ears' also produces very few flowers and earns admiring glances with its jumbo foliage.

(145) **Cranesbills are invaluable—their attractive leaves cover the roses' knobby knees, and their sprays of profuse flowers are just the right size and color to enhance the rose blossoms.** Blue-violet *Geranium ibericum* flowers for six weeks in midspring just as the pink, velvety red, and white old roses open. Flowering for most of the summer, *Geranium* 'Wargrave Pink' is a sweet companion for the later Bourbon, rugosa, and hybrid musks. I like three-foot-tall *Geranium nodosum* at the base of leggy shrub roses and climbers—its

shiny leaves and pale lilac flowers camouflage awkward canes. Knee-high *Geranium sanguineum* 'Album' is attractive at the base of nearly any rose—its daintily dissected leaves and pure white flowers never fail to please.

146 *Geranium* **'Mrs. Kendall Clarke' is a perfect foil for vigorous old roses.** Grown in a border by itself, 'Mrs. Kendall Clarke' swells into a billowing mound, two and a half feet tall and equally wide, and then collapses and topples over in the spring rains. Grown at the base of old roses, it can lean comfortably against roses' ankles as its smoky blue-gray flowers weave into the lower branches. I like the muted flowers equally well with velvety red 'Alain Blanchard', white 'Madame Hardy', and pale pink 'Great Maiden's Blush'.

147 **Where you need an evergreen carpet at the base of roses, rely on** *Geranium macrorrhizum* **and its cultivars.** Blooming ahead of the roses in early spring, *Geranium macrorrhizum*'s bright pink flowers are enlivening, but it's the lobed evergreen leaves that are so valuable for carpeting bare stretches of the ground in winter. For those who prefer white, there's *Geranium macrorrhizum* 'Album'. Other choices abound: light pink 'Ingwersen's

Variety', pink 'Lohfelden', and magenta 'Czakor', to name a few.

148 **Plant drought-tolerant flowering herbs in sunny beds to help out the bare ankles of climbing roses.** Billowing mounds of lavender and catmint (*Nepeta x fassenii*) do wonders to camouflage the woody base of climbing roses while adding extra color and fragrance. Low hedges may be made entirely of lavender or catmint to lend a formal structural edging to a rose bed. Picture their spikes of purple flowers in full bloom, uniting a colorful array of roses.

For later in summer, the purple flowers of 'Hopley's Purple' oregano and airy sprays of lavender Russian sage (*Perovskia atriplicifolia*) add zest to rose borders.

149 **Try fancy-foliaged sages for a showy edging at the base of shrub roses.** Purple sage makes a smashing accent near pink or red roses, while golden sage flatters yellow roses, echoing their color, and complements red roses as well. The tricolor sage with touches of pink and cream is effective with pink or white roses nearby.

150 **Rosemary and rue add foliage color and texture to rose bor-**

ders. I love deep green upright 'Arp' rosemary in front of shrubby roses. The needle-like evergreen leaves are handsome and smell heavenly when crushed, and the blue flowers are wonderful with any color rose. It's a pleasure to harvest an occasional stem for the kitchen during the summer and dry a whole bunch in the fall, enough to last all winter.

Equally attractive, 'Jackman's Blue' rue can be planted as a low hedge in front of roses. The blue-green leaves are cooling and handsome, topped by small yellow flowers in early summer. Wear waterproof gloves and be very careful when pruning rue—the sap can be irritating to your skin and eyes.

(151) At the base of roses that are well clothed with leaves, try a carpet of drought-tolerant, low-growing sedums. My friend Donna Freeman planted evergreen *Sedum spurium* at the base of a hedge of 'Fru Dagmar Hastrup' rugosa roses. The waxy, succulent leaves of this pink-flowering sedum make a handsome ground cover tough enough to smother weeds and reduce maintenance beneath the roses.

Or try *Sedum kamtschaticum*, with bright green leaves and yellow flowers in late summer. Dusky-leaved *Sedum* 'Vera Jameson' and gray-green *Sedum sieboldii* are trailing succulents that bloom in the fall, along with *Sedum* 'Ruby Glow' and *Sedum* 'Rosy Glow'.

152 **Plant silver-foliaged wormwood (*Artemisia*) in front of roses for an elegant effect.** Gray leaves have a soothing effect in the garden and are especially welcome to enhance red, orange, and pink roses. In a white garden they add a subtle touch to the limited color palette without distracting from the mood of serenity.

Silvery *Artemisia* 'Valerie Finnis' is nearly white on a sunny day, its gray bloom spikes more texturally interesting than flowery. *Artemisia pontica* is more of a gray-green and feathery in texture. *Artemisia* 'Huntington' and *Artemisia* 'Powys Castle' make rounded, billowing mounds the size of small shrubs and are excellent for softening the base of woody shrub roses or climbers. In front of smaller roses, let *Artemisia canescens* sparkle–its asymmetrical branches are a filigree of silvery foliage.

153 **Common self-seeding annuals and biennials make great companions at the base of old roses.** It's not much fun to garden at the base of prickly old roses, so the self-sowers spare you the work. Feverfew, columbines, love-in-a-mist (*Nigella*), and forget-me-not are easy and colorful.

Once they're planted, they'll disperse their own seed and die back under the roses as a natural mulch. If you want to tidy up, just rake out their spent foliage in the fall with a long-handled leaf rake.

To limit the spread of self-sowing annuals and biennials, cut off the dead heads before the seeds disperse. You may find that some self-sowers are too aggressive for the size of your garden—if so, deadhead all but a few of the flowers (these few will self-sow for next year) as soon as they are spent to prevent them from going to seed.

154 Dianthus of many kinds are good friends for roses. Perennial cottage pinks (*Dianthus plumarius*) spread in silvery carpets at the feet of roses, perfuming the air with their clove-scented flowers when they bloom in spring. All they need is a little bonemeal and a good haircut after they bloom to keep them compact. My favorite of all is 'Inchmery', a silvery pink with strong fragrance.

Biennial Sweet William (*Dianthus barbatus*) will return each year if you let the flowers go to seed and sprinkle the black seeds back into the beds where you'd like them to return. Their pink, red, magenta, white, and burgundy flowers are in total harmony with the color spectrum of the old roses. They too are scented.

Annual *Dianthus* hybrids are a good accompaniment for midsummer's reblooming roses. In shades of pink, red, violet, salmon, and white, you'll find them in nurseries with names like 'Princess', 'Magic Charms', and 'Parfait'.

Dianthus are easy to start from seed indoors before the start of the garden season or outdoors as soon as the soil warms up.

(155) **Medium-height bellflowers are wonderful companions in front of taller roses or between medium-sized shrubs.** Bellflowers bloom in blue and in white, perfect colors for red, pink, magenta, or even white and yellow roses. *Campanula latifolia*, with lovely tubular flowers pointing sideways off the four-foot stems, is early enough for the spring-blooming old roses. *Campanula persicifolia* and *Campanula latiloba*, with columns of bell-shaped flowers facing outward all along the stem, bloom in time for summer's hybrid musks, shrub roses, and Bourbons. *Campanula lactiflora*, with all its flowers in a cloud at the tops of the stems, is best used in front of or between shrub roses.

(156) **Sea kale (*Crambe cordifolia*) provides a splendid backdrop for a shrub rose.** Picture a baby's breath

that blooms six feet tall with basal leaves that look like rhubarb—that's about the way sea kale looks. Place it behind a shrub rose and its veil-like white flowers will flatter the roses just as baby's breath does in a big bouquet. The best example I ever saw was at Kinzy Faire, Millie Kiggins' and Penny Vogel's garden in Estacada, where a huge sea kale was blooming behind 'Sharifa Asma', a very fragrant English rose. 'Sharifa Asma' is a blend of pastel pink and creamy white, like pink icing and whipping cream. Together with the sea kale it made an ethereal sight.

157 Lacy white flowers will flatter just about any color rose. Whether a rose is velvety red or satiny pink, a touch of lacy white flowers at the shrub's hem will add interest and complement the roses. Try annual bishop's flower (*Ammi majus*), which looks very much like Queen Anne's lace, only shorter and more refined, a filigree of tiny, pure white flowers. The white form of Jupiter's beard (*Centranthus ruber* 'Alba') fills in nicely at the base of woody roses with spikes of off-white flowers. So does the white form of moss campion (*Lychnis coronaria* 'Alba'), with small circular flowers atop gray foliage.

Waist-high *Gaura lindheimerii*, with flower spikes that begin coloring up in June and continue until frost, is an exceptionally long-blooming perennial that multiplies rapidly by seed. And low-growing Santa Barbara daisy (*Erigeron karvinskianus*) billows nicely at the base of roses with small but profuse flowers that are pink fading to white. Of course all of these flowers are excellent for a white garden.

158 **Plant long-lasting summer-blooming perennials in front of and between reblooming roses to fill the gaps.** *Aster x frikartii*, loaded with blue daisies from July to frost, is about three feet tall, just high enough to camouflage knobby rose knees. Be patient with this perennial, as it leafs out late and takes a few years to come into its fullness. Pink and white mallows (*Malva alcea fastigiata* and *Malva moschata*) blend beautifully with roses in similar hues. Cut the spent flowers off and you'll be rewarded by two or three further bloom periods.

159 **For a more contemporary style, combine roses with ornamental grasses.** The linear leaves of ornamental grasses give a crisp geometric look to a border. Try blue oat grass (*Helictotrichon sempervirens*) in front of a pink shrub rose such as 'Bonica' or at the edge of 'Scarlet Meidiland'. Try a few drifts of the 'Red Baron' bloodgrass

(*Imperata cylindrica* 'Red Baron') at the base of a yellow rose such as 'Golden Wings' or 'Windrush' or to bring out the red in 'Parkdirektor Riggers'.

To enhance white roses, try a clump of variegated grass nearby—*Miscanthus sinensis* 'Variegatus' has narrow, white-striped leaves that echo the white flowers. Yellow-striped zebra grass (*Miscanthus sinensis* 'Zebrinus') similarly would echo yellow roses.

160 Tall annuals make quick filler between newly planted bush roses. Whenever I start a new border, I let cosmos and spider flower (*Cleome*) help thicken the planting. This is especially important when planting own-root roses that start out not much larger than a few pencils. Cosmos and spider flower both come in an assortment of pink, white, and violet shades and produce very satisfying bouquets of flowers in the garden and for cutting, all in one season. Not only that, but they self-sow and return as reliably as perennials—just be careful to identify the cosmos and spider flower seedlings as you're cleaning up in spring, and don't weed them out by accident.

As the roses spread and cover more ground, thin out the annuals accordingly, and move them to newer beds that need help.

161 **Plant medium-height annuals in front of developing roses to add interest.** White flowering tobaccos, large-leaved *Nicotiana sylvestris* and *Nicotiana* 'Jasmine', are both lovely with roses, wafting fragrance into the garden at dusk. I get a kick out of the green bells of *Nicotiana langsdorfii* and chartreuse *Nicotiana* 'Lime Green'—add some 'Envy' zinnias and bells of Ireland to keep the green going.

Salvia 'Victoria' is a very popular annual, offering generous blue spikes all summer long. And most folks stop in their tracks to admire pincushion flowers, old-fashioned annuals that bloom in an assortment of purple, burgundy, pale blue, and even white, blue, and mauve. A bit spindly, they benefit from leaning on sturdier perennials or annuals.

162 **Carpeting annuals are great to color the ground at the base of roses.** One year I planted a long border of floribunda roses in front of white picket fence for a client and added a mass of sweet alyssum underneath. Simple, white, and fragrant, the sweet alyssum united the roses and pulled them together with the white fence. Swan River daisies with soft, ferny foliage and froths of blue-violet flowers would work well too with almost any color rose.

For a sunny look, try yellow roses underplanted with red-orange tagetes marigolds 'Paprika' or yellow 'Lemon Gem', or try orange *Zinnia angustifolia*, a billowing single-flowered ground cover. Weave in some blue petunias or browallias (bush violet) to cool down the heat.

163 Plant early-flowering onions to accompany the old roses. Flowering onions may not sound very glamorous, but in fact many alliums have surprisingly showy globe-shaped flower heads filled with tiny star-shaped blossoms.

Allium christophii blooms in spring in time to keep company with old roses, peonies, and cranesbills (*Geranium* species and hybrids). The large round silvery lavender flowers bloom atop 18-inch stems like oversized lollipops and fade to the color of straw in summer, still retaining textural interest. The naked stems look best rising up through a billowing perennial, *Geranium ibericum*, for example, with blue-violet flowers and lobed leaves.

Allium aflatunense grows about three feet tall and benefits from a skirt of a two-foot-high, loosely-growing perennial—try the white form of Jupiter's beard (*Centranthus ruber* 'Alba') or honesty (*Lunaria annua* 'Alba'), or silvery 'Powys Castle' artemisia.

White *Allium neapolitanum* is only a foot or so tall and looks sweet and crisp at the front of a border with old roses. The pure white flowers are loosely clustered and make nice additions to bouquets despite their oniony scent.

(164) **Make your rose borders more exotic by adding Byzantine gladiolus (*Gladiolus byzanticus, Gladiolus communis*).** Although summer-flowering glads are far too stiff and ungainly to mix with roses, the slender Byzantine gladiolus is a much more graceful plant. Small tubular flowers of a rich pinkish burgundy color cover the 18-inch stems, which lean at an angle. Blooming in early summer, they make a dark, bright accent at the feet of pink and wine-colored old roses. Surround them with a carpet of blue-violet *Geranium ibericum*–that way the cranesbills' foliage will take over when it's time to deadhead the gladiolus.

The white form, 'Albus', and a cerise form, 'Ruber', may also come in handy. As with most bulbs, more are better. Plant in generous drifts of 25 or more for the best effect. These hardy bulbs are also tolerant of dry situations.

(165) **Add midseason flowering onions for extra color near reblooming roses.** Low-growing *Allium* *azureum* has unusual light blue flowers in early summer. Use it at the edge of the border to add extra color. Taller *Allium* 'Purple Sensation' comes up high enough to meet the roses and mingle with them, about two and a half feet, with dramatic purple flowers that add zing.

The shapely round heads of *Allium multibulbosum* are unusually striking, for each globe is an assembly of dozens of tiny white flowers with green buttons at their centers, making a very pleasing pattern. All in all this flowering onion has a very refined, soothing effect, and combines very well with any color of rose.

Maroon drumstick allium (*Allium sphaerocephalum*) contributes a rich dark hue that is a very welcome accent near pink reblooming roses. The flowers are small, so many bulbs are needed to form a significant drift of color–30 to 50 is not too many.

166 Grow the early-blooming regal-lilies (*Lilium regale*) to accompany old roses. Regal lilies (*Lilium regale*) are a luxurious touch near old roses. Their buds are maroon, opening to large white trumpets with a spicy fragrance. Beautiful in all stages from promising bud to fully open flower, regal lilies provide delightful contrast to the rounded rose shape.

Most lilies are a bit gawky, having narrow stems and oversized flowers. Surround them with a billowing perennial with small subtle flowers, such as baby's breath or *Gaura lindheimerii*, that will billow out around the lilies, like filler in a bouquet.

167 **Add Asiatic lilies near reblooming roses for early summer color.** A profusion of Asiatic lilies are available in orange, peach, pink, yellow, and white. Blooming in June and early July, they make great companions for summer-blooming roses. Keep the pink and cream-colored ones near the pink and reddish pink roses and save the yellow, peach, and orange lilies for warm-toned roses in shades of orange, red, and yellow. 'Côte d' Azur' is one of the best pink Asiatics, excellent for bouquets. 'Brushstroke', a white lily with plum markings, is also very striking.

168 **Try trumpet lilies near summer-blooming roses.** The most opulent summer-blooming lilies are the Aurelian or trumpet lilies that open in July and August. Huge flowers flare out from the stems, weighing them down–staking is usually helpful unless you want to cut the stems for bouquets.

Some favorites: 'Pink Perfection', with deep pink flowers, and 'Golden Splendor', with enormous fragrant blossoms that look sensational near red roses.

Remember that lilies of all sorts require good drainage and protection from slugs, which love to bite off the new buds.

169 Add Oriental lilies to rose borders to extend the color into late summer and fall. Avoid the late summer doldrums by adding Oriental lilies to spice up the roses. Clove-scented and opulent, they bloom in shades of pink, white, and red; some are speckled and banded with unusual patterns to further fascinate us.

Showiest of all is the enormous white Oriental lily 'Casa Blanca', which is sold by florists as an outstanding cut flower. One stem will last for weeks indoors, longer in the garden. White of course flatters any rose. Possibly even more popular, 'Star Gazer' has upward-facing, fragrant, deep crimson flowers edged in white.

Roses for Particular Places

170 Although I sometimes think it's our perverse nature that insists on growing roses in shade, the hybrid musk roses' versatility makes it possible to do just that. I have grown white 'Moonlight' in nearly full shade, where its clusters of semidouble flowers with golden stamens sparkle. 'Ballerina' and 'Felicia' actually bloom better in partial shade–their pastel pink petals stay fresh longer and show up better than in full sun, where they bleach out. White 'Prosperity' tends to turn brown quickly in intense sunlight and stays fresh a lot longer in dappled shade.

171 The vigorous alba roses bloom well in partial shade, making

them good candidates for climbing trees. One of the tough things about training roses up trees is that it's often shady on the way up to the top, and most of us would prefer that the roses bloom along the ascent, where we can see them. 'Belle Amour' does this very well, sending its thorny canes way up into my pear tree and blooming so lustily all the way that folks want to know what that pink tree is.

'Königin von Dänemark' ('Queen of Denmark'), also a pink alba, with quartered flowers, blooms well in a shady area where Austin roses languish for lack of light (they'll be moved next spring).

172 **In dryer beds and borders, choose tougher roses that can manage with less water.** My test bed is invaded by the roots of several preexisting trees and goes bone-dry in summer, despite twice-weekly watering and years of amending the soil. I've had to remove most perennials from this harsh site, yet several roses flourish here. Light pink 'New Dawn', normally a climber, grows as a vigorous shrub (I peg the canes); likewise the magenta rambler, 'Russell's Cottage Rose' (it's still waiting for the gazebo I plan to build some day). A colony of deep pink *Rosa gallica* and its striped sport 'Rosa Mundi' keeps the front of this bed brilliant and fragrant in late spring and early summer.

173 **In sandy soil or dry gardens, take advantage of adaptable *Rosa rugosa.*** Commonly called sea tomatoes because they flourish at the seaside and bear hips resembling bright red cherry tomatoes, rugosa roses are used to growing in sandy sites lacking moisture. Use them where your soil is lean and sandy or where the water is scanty, whether because of competing tree roots or a dry climate. They'll perform just as well in wet climates, so basically they're just plain easy. The closer they are to the species, or wild rugosas, the more carefree–white 'Blanc Double de Couvert', pink 'Fru Dagmar Hastrup', magenta 'Hansa', and pink 'Scabrosa' are just about indestructible. 'Conrad Ferdinand Meyer', a gorgeous rugosa so hybridized that its pink flowers resemble those of a hybrid tea rose, is more susceptible to aphids and rust.

174 **Let the tough Scotch or burnet rose (*Rosa pimpinellifolia, R. spinosissima*) cover the ground where your soil is sandy or dry.** In the wild, burnet roses colonize sand dunes and windswept hillsides. Ferny leaves give them a deceptively delicate look–these are tough customers. The species bear single white flowers followed by dark maroon hips that look almost black. Depending on the richness of the soil and the amount of water, they can grow anywhere from three to six feet tall.

Single and double named forms of the Scotch roses (also called Scots briar) are also available. Some popular burnets are single pink 'Mary Queen of Scots' and pastel pink 'Stanwell Perpetual', with double, quartered flowers that rebloom. For a small place, 'William III' is an outstanding shrub, only three by three, with semidouble magenta flowers and a crop of hips the color of bittersweet chocolate.

175 Polyantha roses are great for gardens with limited space. Even if all you have is a small entry garden, make room for some polyantha roses that rebloom all summer. 'White Pet', a fragrant polyantha, is sure to please, with small double white pompom flowers and repeat bloom. Two-foot-tall 'Jean Mermoz' offers an abundance of small perfectly shaped pink roses all summer long. For a deeper color, enjoy blue-purple 'Baby Faurax', first introduced in 1924. 'Cameo' is a refreshing shade of coral and blooms continuously, and 'Margo Koster' is an even deeper, lively blend of orange and pink.

176 Try the compact forms of the reblooming English shrub roses in smaller gardens. 'Mary Rose', a lovely English shrub rose with double pink flowers, stays under four feet tall and spreads about equally wide. 'The Prince' is only about three feet tall, with deliciously fragrant, double, deep red-purple flowers typical of old roses. 'Tamora' is a short, bushy apricot rose with deeply cupped flowers and good fragrance. 'Pretty Jessica' is made for the small garden, with warm pink flowers, good perfume, and the looks of an old rose. So is 'Wife of Bath', with small rose-pink cupped flowers and good repeat bloom.

177 Several hybrid musks are fine for smaller gardens. Silvery pink 'Felicia', with double flowers that look like miniature hybrid tea roses, is slender and upright in form, about three feet across and four feet tall. 'Prosperity', a double white hybrid musk, is a little taller but doesn't spread much more than four feet across. And creamy pink 'Penelope' also takes only four feet of width and is just about that tall too.

178 If you're short on space, choose floribundas that rebloom well and grow moderately. 'Iceberg' is the best white floribunda for disease resistance, rebloom, and beautiful flowers that repeat well. 'Sunsprite' is a very pleasing clear yellow with shapely flowers and continuous bloom. 'Trumpeter' is a good performer that stays compact, with red-orange flowers.

'Regensberg' is a most unusual floribunda, part of a group known as handpainted roses. The ruffled petals are very bright pink, with white at their centers and on the reverse side, making them even brighter. Shorter than most floribundas, 'Regensberg' is often used as a ground cover, and is certainly fine in a container.

179 **The same roses recommended for growing in smaller gardens may be grown successfully in containers, just as long as you water and feed them frequently.** If you're gardening on a patio, balcony, or deck, you can enjoy roses in pots. Make sure the containers are big (at least 18 inches wide and deep, but bigger is better) and thick walled to protect the roots from extremes of cold and heat. Make sure the pots have good drainage holes to prevent root rot.

Use a rich, well-draining soil mixture and expect to water frequently. I keep my containers close to a hose bib to make the job easier—some gardeners run automatic drip lines to each container for convenient watering.

Stir some slow-release fertilizer into the soil, but keep fertilizer away from new roots to prevent burning—put some plain dirt between the fertilizer and the root zone as a buffer. Occasional dilute solutions of liquid fertilizers give containered roses the extra boost they need to stay in full bloom.

180 **Dennis Konsmo, a prize-winning rose grower in the Pacific Northwest, grows roses in 15-gallon containers using the following formula for success.** Mix up a big batch of soil with 25 percent mushroom compost and 75 percent three-way mix—one-third sand, one-third black topsoil, and one-third bark dust or sawdust. Fill the lower third of the container with this soil mix, and add a cup of each of the following to it and mix thoroughly: fish meal, bonemeal, blood meal, kelp meal, cottonseed meal, triple superphosphate (0-45-0), dolomite lime, and gypsum. Add two shovels of plain soil mix on top of this richly amended soil, to keep from burning the roots. Then place the rose on top, add more soil mix until the pot is full, and water thoroughly.

181 **In colder climates, potted roses need protection.** Since the sides of the pots are exposed to cold and wind, roses in containers are likely to suffer in colder zones. Either plant them in the ground for winter and top-dress them with a few inches of mulch or move them to a sheltered place out of the wind. Storing them in a cold frame or an unheated greenhouse is another option.

182 **Where summers are very hot, double-potting a rose or adding a hydrogel to the soil keeps containers from drying out.** On a garden tour one hot July day when the temperature soared over 100 degrees, a garden owner pointed out a perfectly content shrub planted this way, and it made me think the same could be applied to a rose. The shrub was planted in a container that was then settled into a larger outer container, with plenty of soil between the two. A trailing ground cover was planted in the outer pot to hide the double rim.

Sure enough, soon afterward I came across this passage in Liz Druitt's *The Organic Rose Garden*: "I had excellent results with container gardening in very exposed locations when I placed one pot inside a larger one and filled the air space between them with some form of mulch. The mulch on top covered the edge of the smaller pot so the roses appeared to be growing in the outer pot, but actually had their sensitive roots protected."

183 **To keep contained roses moist, add a hydrogel to the soil and group pots together.** Sold as plant watering crystals, hydrogels look like coarse salt. They absorb water and swell up, forming a substance like Jell-O. Since pots dry out a lot faster than garden beds, especially when they're made of porous clay, hydrogels slow down the water loss and keep the pots damp a lot longer than normal.

Grouping pots together makes watering more convenient and also tends to keep all the containers moister, since the ground beneath them stays damp longer from the extra runoff that collects at their feet.

184 **Roses that drape are especially graceful in containers.** Much as I love 'The Fairy', a sweet pink polyantha rose with profuse small double flowers, its cascading form was all wrong for the big mixed border where it was growing. It looked lost between all the bigger roses and perennials, and instead of being graceful, its arching branches seemed floppy and dumpy. In despair, I dug it up and planted it in a huge container, thinking I would give it away, but soon it spilled over the edges and all but hid the pot in an avalanche of pink flowers. I found it much more satisfying in a container and ended up keeping it.

'Raubritter', a once-blooming hybrid macrantha with double cupped pink flowers, also tends to drape. In a pot or raised bed, this fountain effect is more graceful than in a conventional border, where the plant appears to be collapsing.

Roses for Every Purpose

185 **Where you need summer privacy, a flowering hedge of tall roses is so much more delightful than privet.** In a place that you mainly view in summer, consider a privacy screen of reblooming roses for a wall of color from late spring through fall. The taller rugosas, such as 'F. J. Grootendorst', full of small double red roses that look like carnations, or its sport, 'Pink Grootendorst', are excellent. 'Hansa', a double, bright pink, and very fragrant rugosa, makes an impenetrable thicket, with big red hips that follow the flowers.

Many of the shrub roses make fine hedges, especially showy 'Westerland', with double apricot flowers that are scented and lovely in bouquets. 'New Face', with sprays of single pink flowers brightened by cream-colored centers, and vivid pink semidouble 'Lyric' are both outstanding.

186. Many of the species roses are ideal for informal screening, reaching eight feet tall and more. The tall, arching canes of *Rosa moyesii* and its near hybrids, 'Sealing Wax', 'Geranium', and 'Highdownensis', are covered with single pink flowers in spring and bright red flagon-shaped hips in summer and fall, adding up to long-lasting interest.

Rosa californica plena also makes a very attractive hedge or windbreak, loaded with fragrant semidouble pink flowers in spring and early summer and covered with small, dark green leaves. It's a vigorous grower that establishes well quickly. Remember that species, or wild, roses are less likely to be affected by diseases or pests than more highly hybridized roses—they're used to surviving without our fussing over them.

187. Where you need a medium-sized hedge or screen, plant four-to-five-foot-tall shrub roses about four feet apart. Sometimes it's useful to plant a four-to-five-foot hedge to separate one garden space, say the vegetable garden or the cutting garden, from the main lawn and borders. Or imagine that you'd like a garden arch to frame a view or invite you into a secret garden—a medium-sized hedge to either side of the arch is useful to clearly define the space.

A vast number of roses could be used for this purpose. I suggest the following for their health and good rebloom quality: 'Iceberg' (white floribunda), 'Bonica' (pink shrub), 'Cornelia' (coral hybrid musk), 'Danae' (creamy yellow hybrid musk), 'Red Glory' (red shrub), and 'Fru Dagmar Hastrup' (pink rugosa).

188 For mixed borders, plant roses that like company, bloom well, and are the right size to make a statement. I like mixing roses with perennials and have found that some do a lot better than others. The wide-spreading hybrid musk roses, especially 'Cornelia', 'Ballerina', and 'Mozart', are excellent. They rebloom well, stand about four to five feet tall and spread equally wide, and don't mind sharing the border with perennials. 'Danae', 'Penelope', and 'Lavender Lassie' also hold their own very well. To my eye, the relaxed way that their flowers bloom in clusters makes their appearance very compatible with perennials.

Several of the medium-sized shrub roses excel in the mixed borders—

'Bonica', 'Pink Meidiland', 'Scarlet Meidiland', 'Red Coat', 'Mary Rose', 'Carefree Wonder', and 'Carefree Beauty' are some good bets.

(189) Use low-growing polyantha, miniature, and short floribunda roses to edge a patio or frame a border. At the edge of a sunny patio, low-growing roses can form a colorful frame all summer just as long as you deadhead the spent flowers. I like 'Jean Mermoz' for its shiny foliage as much as the adorable pink flowers, and 'Cupcake', an award-winning pink miniature rose.

Short roses can define the edge of a border while adding color and fragrance. 'Mr. Bluebird' is a miniature with unusual blue-violet flowers—imagine it planted as a low, reblooming hedge at the feet of pink shrub roses such as 'The Countryman' or 'Mary Rose'.

(190) Although there are plenty of flowers that rival the beauty of roses—iris, peonies, lilies—none can replicate the perfume of a rose. Graham Stuart Thomas points out that roses were grown principally for scent at first, and that fragrance accounts for their lasting appeal. That intoxicating quality gives us so much pleasure and surrounds us with sweetness. Invariably when I visit a rose nursery, I notice people stopping to sniff. When the aroma is fragrant, they put their nose back in the rose for a second whiff, but when there's no scent they look disappointed.

Some especially fragrant roses: 'Ispahan' (damask), 'La Ville de Bruxelles' (damask), 'Celestial' (alba), 'William Lobb' (moss), 'Conrad Ferdinand Meyer' (rugosa), 'Roseraie de l'Hay' (rugosa), 'Hansa' (rugosa), *Rosa rugosa* 'Blanc Double de Couvert', 'Madame Isaac Pereire' (Bourbon), 'Zephirine Drouhin' (Bourbon), 'Vanity' (hybrid musk), 'Nur Mahal' (hybrid musk), 'Lavender Lassie' (hybrid musk), 'Gertrude Jekyll' (English shrub), 'The Prince' (English shrub), 'Othello' (English shrub), 'Sharifa Asma' (English shrub), 'New Dawn' (climber), 'Veilchenblau' (rambler), 'Perfume Delight' (hybrid tea), 'Mrs. Oakley Fisher' (hybrid tea), 'Mr. Lincoln' (hybrid tea), 'Fragrant Cloud' (hybrid tea), 'Margaret Merril' (floribunda), 'Sunsprite' (floribunda), 'Angel Face' (floribunda).

The degree of scent that you experience depends on the temperature and the humidity. The best temperature for the roses' fragrant oils to release into the air is about 65 to 70 degrees, with the sun shining. On very hot days the fragrant oils will burn off and you won't be able to detect as much perfume by the afternoon. Humidity also holds the fragrance in the air and keeps it fresh.

Some roses exude stronger fragrance in springtime, while others reach their full scent in the fall. 'Cornelia' seems sweetest to me in the spring, while 'Vanity' pours out a powerful scent in the autumn, spicy and sweet like sweet peas.

191 Thornless climbers are easier on the gardener and especially useful near seating areas. Even though I treasure 'New Dawn' when it smothers my arbor with pink, fragrant flowers, I must cut off its jagged thorns along canes that come dangerously close to built-in benches beneath the arbor. In situations like this, thornless climbers are much more suitable—just remember that without thorns as hooks that help the rose grab and hold onto a structure, you may have to do a little more training and tying.

'Zephirine Drouhin', a bright pink, fragrant Bourbon rose, has very long, smooth canes that are a pleasure to train—no thorns at all to snag you. Grow it as a shrub or give it a trellis to climb. 'Kathleen Harrop' is the pastel pink sport of 'Zephirine Drouhin', with a very similar growth habit and thornless canes.

The rambler 'Violette' is nearly thornless, with good leaves and clusters of maroon-violet flowers with contrasting yellow stamens and very pliable canes.

In warmer climates, Lady Banks's rose, hardy to zones 8–10, is a good choice. The white-flowering *Rosa banksiae banksiae* is scented, while the yellow form, *Rosa banksiae lutea*, lacks fragrance but is equally popular. Both are strong growers, suitable for covering an arbor or shed in just a few years.

The very popular English shrub rose 'Heritage', with double pastel pink flowers and a light fragrance, also has few thorns on its smooth, flexible canes. Tall enough for the back of the border, 'Heritage' can also be trained to climb.

192 **For a fall and winter bonus, choose from the many species roses that form colorful hips.** At Sissinghurst in September, a hedge of *Rosa virginiana* stopped me in my tracks. Loaded with shiny red hips, it drew me into a garden room full of fall-flowering companions in warm colors—yellow *Clematis orientalis* and orange California fuchsia (*Zauschneria californica*). In mixed borders nearby, repeated plantings of *Rosa moyesii* 'Geranium', full of flagon-shaped red-orange hips, were as colorful as the blue 'Wonder of Staffa' asters (*Aster x frikartii* 'Wonder of Staffa') that billowed at their feet.

Tools for Pruning and Other Helpful Hardware

(193) **Always carry a pair of Felco #2 hand pruners at your side for deadheading, pruning, and cutting flowers.** Invest in a pair of Felco #2 hand pruners and a sheath that you can slip onto your belt and you will always be ready to prune and groom your roses. The blades cut clean without crushing the stems and the handles have grooves to fit your hand perfectly. Best of all, carrying your pruners in a holster frees up your hands and insures that you won't misplace your pruners somewhere in the jungle.

194 Make sure you own a pair of long-handled loppers, the better to reach down into dense, shrubby roses. My favorite loppers are Corona #324, with three-inch blades, long enough to cut through tough wood and curved like talons to grip the base of a shrub rose cane at ground level. Its aluminum handles are lighter than wood, easing the stress on my arms. The handles are 20 inches long, and the overall tool lets me reach safely two feet further into the middle of thorny shrubs.

195 Keep a small folding saw handy for pruning extra-thick rose canes at the base of old plants. Don't wreck your hand pruners or your loppers trying to prune seriously thick woody rose cancs. Purchase a small folding saw, and grab it to do heavy pruning. The one I like best is called an ARS pull saw—its sharp jagged teeth do the job every time.

196 Label your roses with permanent markers. If the rose bug bites you hard, it's easy to lose track of the names. Labels identify them for your own mental clarity and make things easy on curious visitors. Zinc rose markers will last longer than plastic ones, which become brittle and break. Be sure to order a permanent carbon marking pencil when you order your labels. The print may fade after a few years of weathering, so you may have to rewrite them eventually. Another even more permanent labeling method is to engrave aluminum markers with an engraving tool or a ballpoint pen. The following companies sell metal rose markers:

Paw Paw Everlast Label Company, PO Box 93-C, Paw Paw, MI 47079;

Eon Industries, Inc., PO Box 11, Dept 1, Liberty Center, OH 43532.

(197) Make a rose map to protect yourself against broken or lost labels. Maybe it's the elves or the birds or my cats, but somehow labels disappear mysteriously. Drawing a rose map proved to be the best strategy for me. It's not a blueprint, just a sketch of the garden beds with the roses listed by location. Now I have a record that's easy to copy and share with visitors.

(198) Peg down arching shrub roses to multiply your flowers and add grace to the plant. If you let shrub roses reach for the sky you'll get flowers only at the tops of their vertical branches. By pulling the branches sideward, you force the rose to break new growth all along the stem instead of just at the tips.

Whether you cut wire coat hangers into short sections and bend them into hairpin shapes or buy ready-made pegging stakes (picture a miniature shepherd's crook made of heavy gauge wire, about 20 inches long, that hooks over the cane and then pins it into the ground), the basic idea is to bend the long main rose canes horizontally into an arched shape and secure the ends to the ground. You can even pound some stakes into the ground and tie the rose canes to the stakes, or anchor the end of the cane with a heavy rock. Any of these methods encourages blooming side shoots to break all along the length of the cane, like a garland.

(199) To avoid staining your wooden structures with rusting hardware, use galvanized wire and galvanized box nails to train climbing roses on the side of your house, garage, or shed. Construct a frame out of 8- or 16-penny galvanized nails and wire. Drive the nails into the siding in the pattern you desire (an arch or the top three sides of a rectangle) and wrap the wire around the nails, then loosely tie the rose canes to the wire with twine.

(200) On a brick surface, use screw-eye hooks and wire to construct

a support for roses. If you're training roses onto a brick house or wall, sketch the shape of your wire support with a pencil, then drill holes along this sketch in the brick or the mortar. Insert screw-eye hooks, run the wire through the eyes, and *voilà*, you have a frame to which you may tie the rose canes.

Suggested Reading

Allison, Sally. *Climbing and Rambling Roses*. Milford, Auckland: Moa Becket Publishers Limited, 1993.

Austin, David. *The Heritage of the Rose*. Woodbridge, Suffolk: The Antique Collector's Club, 1988.

Barton, Barbara J. *Gardening by Mail*. Boston: Houghton Mifflin Company, 1994.

Beales, Peter. *Classic Roses*. New York: Holt, Rinehart and Winston, 1985.

Beales, Peter. *Twentieth Century Roses*. London: Collins Harvill, 1988.

Dobson, Beverly and Peter Schneider. *Combined Rose List 1997*. Mantua, OH: self-published (available from Peter Schneider, POB 677, Mantua, OH 44255).

Druitt, Liz. *The Organic Rose Garden*. Dallas: Taylor Publishing Company, 1996.

Fearnley-Whittingstall, Jane. *Rose Gardens*. New York: Henry Holt and Company, 1989.

Fisher, John. *The Companion to Roses.* Topsfield, MA: Salem House Publishers, 1987.

Griffiths, Trevor. *The Book of Old Roses.* London: Michael Joseph Limited, 1984.

Griffiths, Trevor. *The Book of Classic Old Roses.* London: Michael Joseph Limited, 1987.

McKeon, Judith C. *The Encyclopedia of Roses.* Emmaus, PA: Rodale Press, Inc., 1995.

Phillips, Roger and Martyn Rix. *Roses.* New York: Random House, 1988.

Phillips, Roger and Martyn Rix. *The Quest for the Rose.* New York: Random House, 1993.

Scanniello, Stephen, Guest Editor. *Easy-Care Roses.* New York: The Brooklyn Botanic Garden, Inc., 1995.

Thomas, Graham Stuart. *The Graham Stuart Thomas Rose Book.* Portland, OR: Sagapress/Timber Press, 1994.

Thomas, Graham Stuart. *The Art of Gardening with Roses.* New York: Henry Holt and Company, 1991.

Toogood, Alan. *Roses in Gardens.* Topsfield, MA: Salem House Publishers, 1987.

Warner, Christopher. *Climbing Roses.* Chester, CT: The Globe Pequot Press, 1987.

Mail-Order Sources for Roses

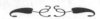

This is just a short list to get you started. For more complete listings, please see Beverly R. Dobson and Peter Schneider's *Combined Rose List 1995*, or Barbara J. Barton's *Gardening by Mail.*

The Antique Rose Emporium, Route 5, Box 143, Brenham, TX 77833, 409-836-9051, 800-441-0002, Fax: 409-836-0928, catalog $5.

Blossoms & Bloomers, East 11415 Krueger Lane, Spokane, WA 99207, 509-922-1344.

Edmunds' Roses, 6235 SW Kahle Road, Wilsonville, OR 97070, 503-682-1476, Fax: 503-682-1275.

ForestFarm, 990 Tetherow Road, Williams, OR 97544-9599, 503-846-7269, catalog $3.

Greenmantle Nursery, 3010 Ettersburg Road, Garberville, CA 95542, 707-986-7504, list available for legal-sized stamped, self-addressed envelope.

Hardy Roses for the North, Box
2048, Grand Forks, B.C. V0H 1H0,
Canada, or Box 273, Danville, WA
99121-0273, 800-442-8122,
catalog $3.

Heirloom Old Garden Roses, 24062
Riverside Drive NE, St. Paul, OR
97137, 503-538-1576,
Fax: 503-538-5902, catalog $5.

Heritage Rose Gardens, Rosequus,
40350 Wilderness Road, Branscomb,
CA 95417, 707-984-6959,
catalog $1.50.

Hortico, 723 Robson Road, Rural
Route 1, Waterdown, Ontario L0R
2H1, Canada, 905-689-6984,
Fax: 905-689-6566.

Jackson & Perkins Co., One Rose
Lane, Medford, OR 97501-0702,
800-872-7673.

Justice Miniature Roses, 5947 SW
Kahle Road, Wilsonville, OR 97070,
503-682-2370.

Lowe's Own-Root Roses, 6 Sheffield
Road, Nashua, NH 03062,
603-888-2214, catalog $2.

Oregon Miniature Roses, Inc., 8285
SW 185th Avenue, Beaverton, OR
97007-5742, 503-649-4482,
Fax: 503-649-3528.

Pickering Nurseries, Inc., 670
Kingston Road, Pickering, Ontario
L1V 1A6, Canada, 905-839-2111,
Fax: 905-839-4807, catalog $3.

John Ellesley Wayside Gardens, 1
Garden Lane, Hodges, SC 29695-0001,
800-845-1124.

White Flower Farm, POB 50,
Lichtfield, CT 06759-0050,
203-496-9600, Fax: 203-496-1418.

Index

‑‑‑ℰᎦ ‑‑‑

Please note: The numbers below re‑ fer to the tips, not to the book's pages.

A

air circulation, 20
alba roses, 30, 58, 78–81, 171
Alchemilla mollis, 144
alfalfa meal, 10
alfalfa tea, 9
Allium
      'Purple Sensation' 165
      A. aflatunense, 163
      A. azureum, 165
      A. christophii, 163
      A. multibulbosum, 165
      A. neapolitanum, 133
      A. sphaerocephalum, 165
alyssum, sweet, 98
Ammi majus, 157
annual bishop's flower (*Ammi majus*), 157
annuals
      carpeting, 162
      medium‑height, 161
      self‑seeding, 153
      tall, 160
aphids, 20, 110
'Arp' rosemary, 150
Artemisia, 63, 152
      'Huntington' 162
      'Powys Castle' 152
      'Valerie Finnis' 152
      A. canescens, 162
      A. pontica, 162
asiatic lilies, 167

Aster x *frikartii*, 158
'Monch' 136
'Wonder of Staffa' 192
Austin roses, 171

B

baby's breath, 166
baking soda solution, 21
Baptisia australis, 136
bark dust, 180
bellflowers (*Campanula* spp.), 52, 155
bells of Ireland, 161
biennials, self-seeding, 153
'Big Ears' lamb's ears, 144
black spot, 21, 101, 110
blood meal, 9, 180
blue oat grass (*Helictotrichon sempervirens*), 159
bonemeal, 1, 10, 180
Bourbon roses, 58, 99, 100, 191
browallias, 162
'Brushstroke' asiatic lily, 167
Buddleia davidii, 48
burnet rose, 55, 174
bush roses, 160
bush violet (*Browallia*), 162
butterfly bush (*Buddleia davidii*), 48
butterfly rose (*Rosa chinensis* 'Mutabilis'), 90
Byzantine gladiolus, 164

C

cabbage roses, 82
California fuchsia (*Zauschneria californica*), 192
Campanula
   C. glomerata, 136
   C. lactiflora, 155
   C. latifolia, 68, 155
   C. latiloba, 155
   C. persicifolia, 155

'Golden Splendor' trumpet lily, 168
grandiflora roses, 44
gray-foliaged plants, 63, 78
greensand, 10
gypsum, 10, 180
'Gypsy Queen' clematis, 136

H
hedge roses, 185–187
Helictotrichon sempervirens, 159
herbicides, 22
hips, rose, 60, 192
honesty (*Lunaria annua* 'Alba'), 163
hybrid musk roses, 52, 103–107, 177
hybrid perpetual roses, 91
hybrid roses, old, 58
hybrid rugosa roses, 30
hybrid tea roses, 44, 52
hydrogel, 182, 183

I
Imperata cylindrica 'Red Baron' 159
'Inchmery' dianthus, 154
'Ingwersen's Variety' dianthus, 147

J
'Jackman's Blue' rue, 150
Jupiter's beard (*Centranthus ruber* 'Alba'),
        157, 163

K
kelp meal, 180

L
lacewings, 20
ladybugs, 20
lady's mantle (*alchemilla mollis*), 144
lamb's ears (*Stachys lanata*), 63, 144
late-blooming roses, 59

Q

quartered roses, 39

R

ramblers, 121–125, 132
reblooming climbers, 122
'Red Baron' bloodgrass (*Imperata cylindrica* 'Red Baron'), 159
Red Damask Rose *see* Apothecary's Rose
Red Rose of Lancaster see *Rosa gallica officinalis*
red-thorned rose (*Rosa sericea pteracantha*), 64
regal lilies (*Lilium regale*), 166
Rosa banksiae banksiae, 191
Rosa banksiae lutea, 55, 191
Rosa beggeriana, 63
Rosa californica plena, 31, 57, 186
Rosa 'Dupontii' 63
Rosa fedtschenkoana, 63
Rosa gallica, 67–73
Rosa gallica officinalis, 37, 57
Rosa gallica versicolor, 57
Rosa glauca, 62, 139
Rosa hugonis, 54
Rosa macrantha, 57, 61
Rosa moschata, 59
Rosa moyesii, 61, 139, 186, 192
Rosa murielae, 51
Rosa nitida, 65, 66
Rosa palustris, 66
Rosa pimpinellifolia, 174
Rosa rugosa, 56, 65, 92–96, 139, 173
Rosa rugosa alba, 56, 190
Rosa sericea pteracantha, 64
Rosa soulieana, 63
Rosa spinosissima, 55, 174
Rosa villosa, 63
Rosa virginiana, 59, 65, 192
Rosa woodsii fendleri, 63
Rosa x *alba,* 63

rose cultivars

V

W

Z